Sensual Orthodoxy

Debbie Blue

Cathedral Hill Press

Sensual
Orthodoxy

Debbie Blue

CATHEDRAL HILL PRESS

Cathedral Hill Press
580 Holly Ave #10
Saint Paul, Minnesota 55102

Art: Jim Larson
Set in Minion Pro 10/12

Printed in the United States of America
  on acid free paper
11 10 09 08 07 06 05 04   4 3 2 1

LCCN 2003-111197
Library of Congress Cataloging-in-Publication Data
Blue, Debbie
  Sensual Orthodoxy / Debbie Blue.
  p.   cm.
  ISBN 0-9742986-0-3
  I. Blue, Debbie II. Title.

Table of Contents

Preface

Imemorized it, carried it dutifully around, I knew it was supposed to be somehow crucial to my life, but there was nothing about the Bible that seemed honestly very intriguing to me. I realized it was prudent to pretend to like it, but it seemed like fairy tales and bedtime stories might actually have more vital clues to the secrets of the universe.

It was presented as something simple and clear. Not thick stories full of twists and tangles and layers, but thin little narratives only perfectly factual. It was about moral instruction. It told us how we were to behave. And the way it got communicated it seemed about as interesting as you might expect an instructor in discipline to be, not wild and passionate and engaged with life, all full of sex and blood and fighting, but neat and prudish and mean and dull. It was a text in the service of some anti-sensual agenda.

How anyone managed to pull that presentation off is fairly amazing. There are monsters in the book. These are graphic stories about people with names and every petty human emotion. It's all about barrenness and fertility and eating. It's full of love and pain and anger and death and all sorts of poetry. It is so not abstract. It is so concrete. It is so many layered.

Somehow, sometimes it seems that believing the Bible is the Word of God can end up making it less instead of more, stiff and dead and thin instead of crazy and full and alive. It may have to do with the people in charge (whether they're scholars or fundamentalists, or ministers of the institution) being so tight about it. It may be something unfortunate that happens with reverence. Reverence and love seem different to me. Reverence is more like distance, Love is engagement.

The Word of God, the word of anybody is the attempt of a live being to communicate something. If God is in any meaningful sense living, then you'd think the Word of God might engage us in a conversation or some sort of relationship rather than hit us like stone tablets falling from the sky. If God is in any meaningful sense alive, then the Word of God wouldn't be like an untouchable repository of facts about God that you must handle barely and gingerly, but something true you could crash around in, actually wrestle with. Wrestling seems like a good way to handle it. Like really handle it. Lots of contact. You might grab it by the neck, yank it around, roll with it in the dirt. Your fingernails won't stay clean. It's not going to break. Instead of approaching it abstractly, we might approach it like a farm wife handles a chicken, carefully but not delicately, thoroughly but not exactly cautiously.

I might be wrong, but what guides my exegesis is the belief that if I hear the Word of God in the struggle it will be the word of a lover. A lover who wants the world to believe in that love and live in that love, not the Supreme Being who wants his subjects lined up properly with their buttons all buttoned right and their shirts clean, their bodies bent in just the right position of supplication. Believing in the living lover at least a little, or in spite of yourself, or starting there even if you don't at the moment believe it that much, makes reading the Bible a pretty interesting adventure. It's different than believing in the possible merits of a religious system, or institution, or moral code. I'm not saying I always do believe that, but it's the hope I entertain (I think that's my job as a pastor, more than, say, promoting the church, or keeping the institution).

Though religion surprisingly often has an anti-sensual, abstracting sort of tendency, the story of Christ goes in the opposite direction. God becomes incarnate, physical, in the world. God is made truly human in the womb of Mary and is born into the world through the birth canal. Jesus Christ walks around and eats and doesn't always wash his hands. God reveals godself as a human with skin and teeth and a tongue, sensing, moving, living, suffering, dying. This is the central story of Christianity and it's a movement to the physical not so much the metaphysical. What I have written here are little stabs at reading the story of Jesus Christ.

These were originally sermons delivered at my church, House of Mercy. They aren't exhortations to a congregation about how they should live their lives. They are attempts to read the Bible with people. And the House of Mercy is an amazing community of people to read the Bible with, up for a struggle and questions, and alive.

Often when I first look at a passage I'm supposed to preach on I get that thing where you cannot make your mind engage with a sentence even though you read it fifty-five times. You keep finding yourself doodling or recalling some conversation or trying to remember what you need from the grocery store. But my process of writing is a process of de-abstraction. I end up getting thoroughly involved. I hope reading them does at least a little of that for you.

Acknowledgements

The first time I actually believed the Bible was interesting or thought that God might really be alive was when I studied with John Linton at the Oregon Extension. I often use the notes from his Bible studies as my commentaries, and they are the funniest, smartest, wildest most interesting commentaries that I have ever encountered. All the best lines, jokes, and readings of the text are probably his. I'm happy to be able to pass them on.

Thanks to Reverend Russell Rathbun for naming the book, titling many of the sermons, and convincing Dan to publish it. Linda Buturian reads all my sermons before I give them. I can't imagine a more helpful and encouraging reader. My husband Jim did the painting on the cover and the drawing of the raven that runs throughout. His paintings are forever informing my sermons and vice versa.

Betty's Manger Scene Collection

January 6, 2002: Epiphany of Our Lord

In the time of King Herod, after Jesus was born in Bethlehem of Judea, wise men from the East came to Jerusalem, asking, "Where is the child who has been born king of the Jews? For we observed his star at its rising, and have come to pay him homage." When King Herod heard this, he was frightened, and all Jerusalem with him; and calling together all the chief priests and scribes of the people, he inquired of them where the Messiah was to be born. They told him, "In Bethlehem of Judea; for so it has been written by the prophet: 'And you, Bethlehem, in the land of Judah, are by no means least among the rulers of Judah; for from you shall come a ruler who is to shepherd my people Israel.'" Then Herod secretly called for the wise men and learned from them the exact time when the star had appeared. Then he sent them to Bethlehem, saying, "Go and search diligently for the child; and when you have found him, bring me word so that I may also go and pay him homage." When they had heard the king, they set out; and there, ahead of them, went the star that they had seen at its rising, until it stopped over the place where the child was. When they saw that the star had stopped, they were overwhelmed with joy. On entering the house, they saw the child with Mary his mother; and they knelt down and paid him homage. Then, opening their treasure chests, they offered him gifts of gold, frankincense, and myrrh. And having been warned in a dream not to return to Herod, they left for their own country by another road. —Matthew 2: 1-12

Betty has a manger scene collection that's staggering. It recalls every nifty craft that's been popular in the last three decades. Cute figures, Furry figures, Scented, Beaded, Glitter, Tie Dye. A couple of years ago Betty displayed a scene where Mary and Joseph appeared to be made out of shellacked marshmallows. But although I find the record of tacky craft show circuit fads fascinating, the really most remarkable thing to me is that all these items (marshmallows, clothespins, sea shells) can be so easily recognized as the Holy Family on Christmas Eve. Just put a beard on a pine cone or a staff in the hands of some rigatonni and we know who it is. We hardly have to look at it, really. We have the scene so thoroughly memorized.

I'm startled by the form of Betty's manger scenes, but never the content. The content is always so entirely predictable—who's there, where they'll stand, what they'll be doing. I'm not sure how it happens that something so full of wild content ends up seeming year after year so unsurprising, so nearly mundane. This is the story about God made flesh in the womb of Mary, God born into the world, as a baby, through the birth canal, in a barn. You'd think we might feel a little shocked every time we encounter it.

I've been thinking maybe someone should start a small group of guerilla activists whose task it would be to plant shocking figures in manger scenes. They could work both inside private homes as well as in the most visible places. Suburban housewives will shriek when they find Batman figures on the roof of the manger on their mantle. Churches will be horrified to find Barbies and plastic dinosaurs on their altars. But people will pay attention. They will look twice. They may even stop their car. They may even get out when they see a garden troll or a pink flamingo or a big plastic Homer Simpson leaning over the baby Jesus on the Cathedral lawn.

I actually wonder if I'm not the first to come up with that idea. It might have been some sort of guerilla group that first placed the wise men in manger scenes. Now, of course, they've been thoroughly appropriated by mainstream crèche manufacturers, but they should really be a more startling presence. It's a little like putting drag queens in the nativity play at Bethlehem Baptist. Their popularly and familiarly known as the wise men or three kings, but they are more properly Magi: magic. They follow stars. They conjure. They are really more Merlin than Arthur. Matthew never suggests that they are kings. They are practitioners in the arts of the occult. Yet year after year they stand there at almost every manger scene all stiff and innocent and respectable as if they fit in, as if they've always been there, as if they're supposed to be there, as if they're not flaming pagans intruding upon the birth scene of a little Jewish family.

These guys probably didn't come from nice clean palaces, maybe not even good families, probably more like smoky little rooms in the back of tattoo parlors or broken down houses full of incense, carnivals, seedy storefronts advertising tarot card readings here, fortunes told, palms read, channel your past life. They are pagans who have been doing pagan things and it was apparently while consulting their pagan astrological charts, that they found a star, evidence in their pagan way of seeing that there had been a birth of a king. And they find Jesus because they follow that light they glimpsed from their far away pagan land.

The astrologers only appear in Matthew, not the other gospels and Matthew doesn't actually have a manger scene. They see the star apparently, when the child is born, then they have a long trip. So it's not actually scripture that places them in our nativity sets. It must have been guerillas.

Matthew does, though, have them figure majorly in his opening scene. In fact it's these magicians, not Mary or Joseph or anyone even remotely in the family, that speak the first human words in Matthew's gospel story. He doesn't give us nice domestic details about the birth. How the baby cooed, what Mary thought when she looked at her new baby. He mentions that Jesus is born practically in passing then shoots right to this pagan entourage sweeping into Jerusalem months later asking "where is he who has been born king of the Jews?"

That's a bold way to tell the story, these foreigners, in every sense of the word, these outsiders (way outsiders) are the first people in Matthew's story to encounter the Jewish Messiah. Talk about being a little bit of a trouble maker or unpredictable or even a revolutionary. We may have thought that our wise men fit so nicely among the shepherds and sheep, but really, it's like having Shirley MacLaine at our manger scene. It's that out there. *Shirley MacLaine*. That doesn't seem that predictable.

I have to say, there's something I like about the thought of my old youth director, Pastor Bob, who loved to preach on the heinousness of paganism and warn us of the evils of astrology, carefully taking those pagan astrologers out of their box every year, and setting them right up next to the Baby Jesus.

The story of the birth of Christ in Luke is all full of angels and songs and warmth and beauty and when I read it, I think, who wouldn't love this little baby Messiah come to bring peace on earth. But Matthew starts out right away *bang* with "tension." You get the outsiders, foreigners, aliens, pagans. You get the immediate story of who wouldn't actually love and want this precious baby messiah. Herod. Herod, who is the king of the Jews, naturally feels his reality is a little bit threatened when the foreign outsiders sweep into his kingdom claiming to have seen the star of the one born king of the Jews. And it's not only Herod that's disturbed, says Matthew, but all of Jerusalem with him.

Well, it does seem like it might be a little disruptive to suddenly have the kingdom of God break into the reality everyone's gotten used to, after all. It seems like there would be maybe a little tension surrounding the emergence of a whole new order. Mostly it seems like there's not really room for another king, a whole different way, and though we don't really have much royalty that rules the world these days, it still doesn't seem like there's exactly much space for this other king, who comes crashing insensibly into the world with all this riffraff in his wake, pagan gypsies with their dancing bears, that whole carnival crowd.

It's disruptive. There's not room for this king and his ways. It doesn't mesh very well with what we know, it's all the wrong shape for any preconceived space. It doesn't fit. I mean how does "love your enemy," or "turn the other cheek," or "blessed are the merciful, the poor in spirit, the meek, and the weak," really, fly in the Pentagon or the White House or your own psyche?

How about "you cannot serve God and Mammon." Does that fit?

I'm not sure if we can really even entertain a compromise with this other king, and his different kingdom. It may sound nice in theory, but it is not compatible with reality, with the mandates of economics, with the interest of the state, with national security, political necessity, big business. It doesn't fit with our evolutionary drives, for pete's sake, to gain, to compete, to succeed, to strive for personal success, to make our own way in the world.

There is no room in the inn, man. We are (it seems to be) thoroughly entrenched in a different paradigm. There is a kingship already present in this world and there's not room for another king. Herod is very clear about this. He is not at all a fool. He discerns the threat immediately and begins the political machinations required to destroy the threat to his reality.

The first thing he does, ironically, is to gather all the religious leaders to help him. He consults the people who know and love scripture the best, asks them for whatever information they can give him about the Christ. They tell him there is a scripture that prophesies that a Messiah will be born in Bethlehem.

Matthew really pushes the tension: on the one hand you have the political leader of God's people, Herod the king, together with the spiritual leaders with the Holy Scriptures, really everything that represents the established order. On the other hand, you have the foreigner, pagan outsiders with their astrological charts, crystal balls, tarot cards, whatever. The scripture-loving religious leaders end up conspiring against their Messiah to have him killed. They don't recognize him. The outsider, pagan sorcerers who get all their information from the stars, recognize the Christ from afar off, and come to worship him.

If you read on in Matthew's story, it becomes pretty clear that his point isn't: we all must become outsiders and pagan magicians. I think this story asks the question, "Is there room for this Christ, for the kingdom of God and all that it brings in its wake?" And it seems like the answer is no. The established order takes offense at Jesus, has no room for Jesus, resists, condemns, seeks to do away with him. And we don't live in this world without being a part of that kingdom, that order, the established reality. There is no room.

Amazingly, the Christ child is born anyway. God is incarnate in the world. There's no conceivable space but God comes. God comes and keeps coming. Christ is born, escapes Herod, makes his way through the royal paradigm, lives, dies at the hands of the "other kingdom" but is resurrected. There's no room for Jesus in the inn, in Herod's kingdom, in the royal paradigm anywhere but that doesn't seem to be much of a deterrence. You can't seal it out. God finds a way in.

Epiphany is the festival that celebrates the universal manifestation of God's light to all people. The wise men represent the miraculousness of what is outside getting in. The light gets in.

Half an Inch of Fiberglass
January 7, 2001: First Sunday of Epiphany

❧

As the people were filled with expectation, and all were questioning in their hearts concerning John, whether he might be the Messiah, John answered all of them by saying, "I baptize you with water; but one who is more powerful than I is coming; I am not worthy to untie the thong of his sandals. He will baptize you with the Holy Spirit and fire. His winnowing fork is in his hand, to clear his threshing floor and to gather the wheat into his granary; but the chaff he will burn with unquenchable fire." So, with many other exhortations, he proclaimed the good news to the people. But Herod the ruler, who had been rebuked by him because of Herodias, his brother's wife, and because of all the evil things that Herod had done, added to them all by shutting up John in prison. Now when all the people were baptized, and when Jesus also had been baptized and was praying, the heaven was opened, and the Holy Spirit descended upon him in bodily form like a dove. And a voice came from heaven, "You are my Son, the Beloved; with you I am well pleased."—Luke 3: 15-22

My in-laws have a cabin on an island in Lake Minnetonka, Minnesota. The only way you can get to it is by boat. When I'm actually on the boat going over, it's usually fairly pleasant and uneventful. But when I anticipate the trip, laying in bed the night before or even in the car on the way there, I inevitably, compulsively imagine that when I'm handing Olivia, my baby, from the dock to the boat, she slips out of my arms into the water. Or I see Miles fall over the edge of the boat and the water closing over his head. Or the boat crashes or capsizes or explodes and I frantically dive and search but my children disappear into the big black lake.

Usually after I've been through that little thought scenario, I briefly think, I'm not going out there. It's too risky. How can we blithely bring our children across miles of a deep dark water, separated from the infinite abyss by only a half an inch of fiberglass, some humanly constructed device probably designed by speed loving water yahoos. Jim can visit his family without us. But I remind myself the kids will have life jackets on and I remember that nifty strap thing on Olivia's jacket that goes between her legs so she can't slip out and if she does fall in, it's designed to hold her head up and the water's not even that deep by the dock and they've never lost one child to the watery depths yet and I realize I'm being unreasonable and insane. And I go to sleep or we go on and it's never actually the least bit scary. Sometimes we even ride around the abyss all day doing water sports.

This compulsive, dread-filled imagination thing never happened before the kids. If I do the thought scenario with just my husband and I, I can stand us on the seats, dance us all around, hang us over the edge even capsize the boat without a speck of gripping dread. I am so thoroughly confident in my own ability to swim that I feel nearly invincible. Surely Jim and I can manage not to drown. But my imagination can barely stand the juxtaposition of my children, the blatantly vulnerable, and the water.

I know rationally, statistically, it's as risky to drive them to the grocery store. But there is something about the boat trip to the little cabin on the little island surrounded by big water that taps into some deep irrational, inexplicable, archetypal thing about water.

I think John the Baptist must have been tapping into that whole thing a little bit, when he was going around baptizing everybody with water. And the church must have been tapping into it too when it almost immediately adopted as its initiation rite baptism by water.

Water is mentioned all over the Bible. It cleanses and purifies. It quenches thirst, and makes everything come to life. It is tears, endlessly flowing, filling the land. It is floods. It is Sheol: the deep dark abyss: hell. It's so many gorgeous things and it's *nothing*. It's beautiful and healing and it's really freaking scary.

Water is formless. It is fluid. If you try to hold it, it slips through your fingers. You can't shape it. You can't pull it and poke it and mold it into what you desire. But according to the mythologies of all sorts of cultures, everything that does have form comes into being by coming out of water. Water is latent potentiality. It is what might or could be. It's full of creative potential: it's out of water that God creates something. But it is also nothing. Chaos, Void, Abyss. It's preexistence: the nothingness before anything was. And it's the nothingness that threatens to dissolve us back into itself. It's death.

In the aquatic symbolism of most cultures, to be immersed into the water is to regress to the preformed state, to dissolve all individual form. It is to be reincorporated into the undifferentiated mode of pre-existence. That may not be bad. That may not be great, but honestly it strikes me as a little scary sounding, not quite in line with what I would consider my long term goals or what I hope to get out of a day.

Water is absolutely essential to existence. Every civilization is built on it or by it. We can't live without it. Our actual physical bodies are something like seventy-five percent water. There's no denying it. It's huge. The symbolic terrain of water is vast: life, death, fear, beauty, creative, terrorizing, sustaining. It's essential. It's redemptive, but it doesn't seem exactly *safe*, maybe.

Baptism by water. What a wild ritual. It may look like no more than getting your forehead wet or dipping in the heated baptismal font. It may seem normal that we dress our babies up and bring them forward smiling, but it's all potentially a bit edgier than that.

Though the water symbolism is all over the Bible (floods, tears, fonts of blessing, ever living life giving streams, dissolution, chaos, the abode of behemoth the devouring sea monster), the story of John the Baptist is really the first mention of baptism in the Bible and as if the storyteller expected the hearers to have some inkling of what baptism by water might be all about, the story doesn't give us a lot of extra interesting information.

We just hear that John the Baptist is out in the water of the river Jordan, baptizing everybody. And the people are taken with it, enthralled, apparently. He has the attention of the multitudes, the text says. The multitudes are apparently so impressed by him, or the baptism, that they start wondering if maybe the baptizer is the Messiah, the long awaited savior of the world.

I wonder what it was exactly that impressed them so. In my experience the ritual has generally not been quite so captivating. People line up politely, waiting to come forward one by one. The baptizer says a few words and then employs either one of two techniques. I learned these recently.

You can dunk someone backwards. For this you have the baptismal candidate clasp their hands together in front of their body as if they are praying or greeting someone in Buddhist fashion. You may want to suggest that they slip one of their hands up a little to hold their nose. It could be embarassing for everybody if the baptismal candidates get water in their nose and come up blowing snot or gasping air. Brace them between your arms, use your knee to balance, and dunk. The other technique is to put your hand on their head and push. Really they do most the work with this technique. It's not like dunking someone who's resisting.

Honestly, like most institutionalized rituals, it doesn't usually quite have the feel of a matter of life and death. Of course something beautiful and meaningful can come of it, but I've never seen it exactly get people all riled up into thinking someone's the messiah or anything.

So, I just wonder if John the Baptist's scene was a little different. Not quite like that ritual technique thing, but maybe a little more dramatic. And edgy. And threatening and beautiful. Life and death-y. Maybe the people were all in the water and there was a strong current flowing around them and it was hard to even stand without being dragged under. So everybody was holding on to each other to keep from being swept away. Mothers were clinging to their children, and John with his crazy hair and locust breath would look around wildly. And there were no lines. People weren't waiting in line. The Baptist would just randomly lunge forward and grab someone and hold them under. Maybe even a little too long. Just when they were about to panic or needed to gasp for air, he'd raise them up.

And maybe it was something you'd never forget because you felt like you'd just survived a plane crash, or a car wreck, or a drowning. You felt the abyss, undifferentiated preexistence, black nothingness, death closing in around you. But then you breathed. Then you were alive. You went under. You actually slipped out of your trusty life preserver if only briefly and then you saw light.

Maybe the whole thing wasn't at all dull-ish, not even all that entirely safe. Maybe it had more of the feel of a matter of life and death. Of course, maybe not. Maybe people did wait in line and the water was calm and John combed his hair and wore a tie for the occasion. Maybe it was all cultured and tame and polite. I don't actually know, but the story of the first baptism does make it clear that the people were impressed by him, this John the Baptist and his baptism. And something moved them to think he might be the messiah.

But John the Baptist says, "No-no-no, look, I baptize with water (not exactly a small, insignificant, safe boring little thing, actually), but the one who comes after me, whose sandal I'm not worthy to untie? He baptizes with the Holy Spirit. If you're impressed by this water ritual, wait," says John "for the baptism he has in store." I'm not sure if this is exactly one of the more calming and comforting portions of the Bible. I get the feeling that baptism isn't like eating candy, doing the back stroke in the Caribbean, being sprinkled with a little warm spring rain. It's hardly the product of piety or devotion.

It's amazing how the church manages to tame the wildest things. What happens when you go under? Or what does it symbolize? If something washes away, what is it? A little dirt on your hands? That not-very-nice-thing you did yesterday? Coming up from the water, are we cleansed from our personal little so-called impurities? I think it may be more like the washing away of all our illusions, what we thought was solid dissolving into the abyss.

We spend most of our time and energy either believing in the life jackets we've elaborately devised, or our ability to swim. Maybe baptism washes away most of what we think our lives depend on, whatever it is we think keeps us afloat: our boats, our brains, our social skills, our money, our careers, our fitness routine, our weapons, our power, the empire.

We give such elaborate attention to devising our life jackets. Perhaps baptism is like shedding those and slipping into the water. Naked. Unprotected. Maybe it's like ceasing to paddle for a minute, giving up the effort to stay dry or being forced to give it up. And for once feeling, or glimpsing, or something, the frightening and beautiful and painful and uncontrollable, really uncontrollable potentiality. It seems like we spend quite a bit of energy dressing ourselves just so, constructing our individual personas, ensuring our personal success, ensuring we're prepared for whatever we imagine the day will bring, devising just the right life jacket to keep us from going under. We believe we can swim, must swim, and life's really a lot about getting good at it.

Maybe Jesus and his holy spirit baptism doesn't even wait for all that to dissolve in the water, but burns it right off our backs with his cleansing fire. Strips us of our illusions, strips us bare, as naked as a baby, blatantly vulnerable. I'm probably wrong to believe in my ability to stay above water. Not probably even, certainly. I'm fooling myself to place so much confidence in my ability to swim. Essentially I'm more like my children than I'm comfortable believing. No matter how much energy I devote to keeping afloat, we're going to go under. The water will close over our head at some point. That's the fact. And no half inch of fiberglass is going to keep me or my children or you from that deep dark water. There is nothing more certain than that.

Baptism stares in the face of this, embraces it, enacts it, then dismisses its seeming finality. Denies that it is pure destruction. Insists that this does not lack hope.

A baptism of repentance for the forgiveness of sins, John the Baptist calls it. Repentance means to completely turn around, to be reoriented in a completely different direction. Maybe the whole staying afloat thing, spending our lives building our boats or rafts, our personal flotation devices, betrays our disorientation. Maybe going under reorients us, sets us to seeing that our life, our existence, doesn't have to be, really isn't about our personal water crafts, our building great, safe, protective outfits.

We usually go about our day believing pretty wholeheartedly that our life jackets will keep us afloat, that, in fact, they are what life is about: It's about whatever keeps us from our essential vulnerability. Maybe baptism frees us to quit living to avoid the deep, to avoid drowning, to avoid being exposed, so always protected. Frees us to slip naked into the water and still hope.

Laboring God

February 28, 1999: Second Sunday of Lent

Now there was a Pharisee named Nicodemus, a leader of the Jews. He came to Jesus by night and said to him, "Rabbi, we know that you are a teacher who has come from God; for no one can do these signs that you do apart from the presence of God." Jesus answered him, "Very truly, I tell you, no one can see the kingdom of God without being born from above." Nicodemus said to him, "How can anyone be born after having grown old? Can one enter a second time into the mother's womb and be born?" Jesus answered, "Very truly, I tell you, no one can enter the kingdom of God without being born of water and Spirit. What is born of the flesh is flesh, and what is born of the Spirit is spirit. Do not be astonished that I said to you, 'you must be born from above.' The wind blows where it chooses, and you hear the sound of it, but you do not know where it comes from or where it goes. So it is with everyone who is born of the Spirit." Nicodemus said to him, "How can these things be?" Jesus answered him, "Are you a teacher of Israel, and yet you do not understand these things? Very truly, I tell you, we speak of what we know and testify to what we have seen; yet you do not receive our testimony. If I have told you about earthly things and you do not believe, how can you believe if I tell you about heavenly things? No one has ascended into heaven except the one who descended from heaven, the Son of Man. And just as Moses lifted up the serpent in the wilderness, so must the Son of Man be lifted up, that whoever believes in him may have eternal life. For God so loved the world that he gave his only Son, so that everyone who believes in him may not perish but may have eternal life. Indeed, God did not send the Son into the world to condemn the world, but in order that the world might be saved through him.—John 3:1-17

You know, you sit down, you try to communicate something about God and all you have are words (if you can even find them) and they're not really very adequate. Maybe you can point in the right direction, but pointing in approximately the right vicinity is about it. Anything I say fails: God isn't *really* light or a father or a mother, or even mercy, love, and wisdom. Because these are just words and what they signify is never the full reality of God.

Really all we have is a bunch of metaphors. And sometimes those metaphors just lie there all flat and limp, meaning nothing to you. Not that you should just throw them away, but maybe they need to be infused with a little imaginative something.

I often have trouble with the journey metaphor. Though it's a very popular metaphor, very widely used—probably one of the best metaphors in the world—still, it's flat for me. When people talk about the Christian journey, when people ask me, "Where's your road leading you these days?" I can only think of Highway 10 which I drive several times a week, or the gravel road that leads to our farm. "My road? Well, it's been a while since the road graders graded it, so it's not so good right now." The metaphor doesn't open up some different way of seeing things, doesn't reveal anything for me.

Obviously this speaks to my own lack of imagination. The possibilities for the journey motif are really endless. There're safaris, and Homeric Odysseys, there's the Magic School Bus, and star trek, and Jack Kerouac On the Road, there're wagon trains, and acid trips. Maybe it's not just simply about straight or narrow or gravel or paved. What is the Christian journey like? This text from John actually infuses the metaphor with some pretty interesting new life, for me, anyway.

Reading this story, it seemed to me that Nicodemus might be looking for a little imaginative possibility. He was a Pharisee, so he probably knew the scriptures backward and forward: all the words, all the metaphors about God ever written. And whatever the godly road was supposed to be back then, I'm sure he walked it. But he's compelled, nevertheless, to seek out this new guy in town, Jesus, who has just been getting some attention for this incredibly disruptive scene he made at the temple and it was Passover (high, important, holy day) and there were pilgrims everywhere trying to attend to their religious journey and Jesus just threw stuff in everyone's path and wrecked everything up.

Nicodemus (the old preserver of the Godly road) is apparently intrigued. He seeks Jesus out and says: "Look, I've been thinking about you and making some observations. I heard about that whole dove thing when you were baptized, and that you turned water into wine, and you made some really bold moves at the temple and I'm beginning to deduce that you must be some kind of teacher of God."

You'd think Jesus would say "You're right. I am." But instead he like whips the rug out from under Nicodemus and sends him flying. He says, "Look, man, you're going down the wrong road, it's not like math. One plus one doesn't exactly equal two. You can't make observations about me and then deduce who I am. You don't *figure out* or *calculate* this whole God thing. The only way you can see the Kingdom of God, really see me..." (and then he says this thing that is so wild) He says, "You must be born again."

That's like, I don't know, like taking things out of the realm of rational discourse. That's like something the king of wizards would say to princes looking for a golden goose or a magic monkey. It's like something out of a fairy tale: "You must be born again." It's like a riddle. It's mysterious. It's wild. And weird. And I hope you can hear it. Because I know this born again thing is potentially sort of shrunk and stuck and dried out like my gravel road.

I think I got a different perspective reading it this time, because birth is not such an abstract thing for me anymore. Once you've actually given birth, you have a heightened awareness of the amazing and colorful and messy details of what it takes for something to be born.

It's incredible, really, that this extraordinary metaphor: "to be born again," could ever get so depleted that it's become equated with a one time, clean little, rational decision somebody makes (or doesn't make) in altar calls, or church camps, or wherever. I mean, c'mon. We're talking about *birthing* and being *born* and that just seems so *unlike* talking about that time when you were six and raised your hand in Sunday school.

Jesus says you have to be *born* again. That seems so different than saying you have to make a decision. I'm not saying there's no place for decisions, I'm just saying this metaphor doesn't seem like the place.

Perhaps my awareness, because I'm a woman who has given birth, is a little more on the side of the birther, but how did we ever take this metaphor and make it all about something the one being born does? I mean who does the most work to get something born?

When Jesus says "unless you're born again you can't see the kingdom of God," it seems to me he's saying, "Nicodemus, you think you've figured something out, but you really have no tools, you have nothing at your disposal—no rational or irrational, mathematical, or artistic means—that is adequate for understanding, for seeing God. For humanity as it is, there's no possibility of seeing or entering the kingdom, you'd have to be *born* again."

Which could almost seem like the equivalent of saying, "Look, it's impossible buddy. Forget it. Go home." Except, Jesus says, "Don't marvel so. Look, it can happen. It does happen. But it's not like something *you* do, or something you even rationally comprehend. It's like the wind. You don't know where it comes from. You can't see it. You surely don't cause it, or make it. You don't set it in motion. You can't even see where it goes. But it blows."

The wind has quite a reputation in the Bible. In Greek and in Hebrew you use the same word for wind, spirit, breath. It's the wind that blew over the primordial chaos to make the world at creation. It's the breath that God blew into the nostrils of Adam to give him life. It's the spirit that blows through the valley in Ezekiel piled high with bones and bones and dry bones, and they rattle, and grow flesh, and stand up.

This being "born again" may not seem like the most likely scenario, but Jesus says: "believe me, trust me, have faith: the wind blows," and the impossible happens, something out of nothing, bones start marching around, and humanity is reborn.

The author says it all so clearly a few paragraphs before our story. He writes, "Children of God are born not of blood, nor of the will of the flesh, nor of the will of man, but of God." Born of God. It seems to me the profundity of the whole born again metaphor lies exactly here. We are being birthed by God. The wind is blowing, and not only blowing, but howling and huffing and puffing like a woman doing Lamaze.

If you look, you can find a lot of interesting sort of birth images in the Bible. God's womb is imagined to be the place where life originated: it was God's womb that birthed the whole world in the first place. There's a Hebrew word used for God's compassion, mercy, love, that can also mean womb: maybe that's the womb that births us. What a nice womb to be born from.

Isaiah talks about the whole complicated history of God with God's people, the history of faith and no faith and brokenness and anger and forgiveness as if the whole time God is this woman laboring with her child, Israel, impatient to deliver it, impatient for it to be born, again.

And for even more birth imagery: There's a Hebrew word for pain in childbearing—it's most often translated as "grieve" in English versions. It's what God is doing as Adam and Eve leave the Garden of Eden. God's grieving, feeling the labor pains for these children. Think about it. If the labor pains were starting way back then? I don't think God's exactly having a picnic birthing humanity...again. Imagine laboring ten thousand years to give birth to your children.

It seems like the popular imagination persists in thinking of God as, I don't know what, some sort of noble stoic man in the sky. Some removed sort of cosmic measurer of righteousness. The impassive patriarch who demands specific sorts of actions before he'll allow people any sort of intimacy, before he'll allow people to be close to him. But scripture really paints such an entirely different picture. Like God *birthing* us. That's sort of intimate from the get go.

This story about being born again has often been reduced to a requirement we must fulfill lest we be eternally damned. That's distorted. I think in this story, Jesus is trying to say—it's part of God's labor for us, with us, that God became human and lived and died on the cross, and through this process which involves God's suffering, humiliation and pain, humanity is born again. And he invites us to believe in this. It's the labor process. In the life, death, and resurrection of Jesus, God brings life to the world. God births children.

Maybe our image of God would be richer if we quit thinking: impassive, stoic, old man on a throne, and imagined a pregnant woman, waddling and crying, yelling from time to time, with the pains of labor, sometimes angry, sometimes tortured—giving birth to her children.

What's it like for the one being born? What's it like for us? What's salvation like? Maybe like being born. Maybe not so much like being in the womb. In the womb, it's warm and dark and soft and cushy. You are very well insulated. Very well protected from the outside world. Not that vulnerable. Your every need is immediately fulfilled. You don't even have to move your mouth to get food. Every desire is immediately gratified. There is no pain.

Then, you're born. Things change. You're immediately prodded and sharp stuff touches you. You can feel cold and suddenly it's possible that you won't get fed the moment you want it. You cry for the first time.

Miles, my son, was around four when I was pregnant with Olivia. He said to me, "I wish I was still in your tummy 'cuz then no one could ever get mad at me." Besides feeling shocked he would articulate such a thing, besides feeling like a wicked evil ogress, besides feeling like I'd been stabbed with a thousand swords, I felt like I wished so much I could recreate the womb for him. Insulate him from the possibility of pain.

Like, "Oh, Miles, I'll never get mad at you again and neither will anyone else if I can help it, and I will remove all toxins from your environment, and dismantle all nuclear warheads, and create world peace, and stop global warming." But actually, I couldn't. And I wouldn't even ever actually wish him back in the womb. I like talking to him too much. I like relating to him as more than a fetus bumping around inside of me.

I think sometimes I imagine salvation is being removed from the possibility of pain and suffering. But that's so much *not* what it's like to be born. As soon as we start that trip down the birth canal, we become vulnerable to all sorts of wonderful and frightening and beautiful and horrible and sad and amazing things.

I feel like this "born again" thing gives us an amazing glimpse at what the Christian journey, the road of salvation, the "walk," might be like: like being born. Not like: doing all the right things, walking a certain way, a straight line, a tight rope, carefully watching your own feet, being attentive to your own road, a journey that requires a map and your ability to follow it.

Maybe we're being born. Again. Maybe the spirit really does move and blow. Maybe it's happening all around us all the time. Maybe God is saving the world. Maybe there's groaning and blood and pain in the birthing process and maybe it doesn't feel like being in the womb. And maybe it isn't always a nice warm breeze but thank God for breath and life and for enduring the labor.

A Potentially Gruesome Metaphor

February 4, 2001: Fifth Sunday of Epiphany

❦

Once while Jesus was standing beside the lake of Gennesaret, and the crowd was pressing in on him to hear the word of God, he saw two boats there at the shore of the lake; the fishermen had gone out of them and were washing their nets. He got into one of the boats, the one belonging to Simon, and asked him to put out a little way from the shore. Then he sat down and taught the crowds from the boat. When he had finished speaking, he said to Simon, "Put out into the deep water and let down your nets for a catch." Simon answered, "Master, we have worked all night long but have caught nothing. Yet if you say so, I will let down the nets." When they had done this, they caught so many fish that their nets were beginning to break. So they signaled their partners in the other boat to come and help them. And they came and filled both boats, so that they began to sink. But when Simon Peter saw it, he fell down at Jesus'ss knees, saying, "Go away from me, Lord, for I am a sinful man!" For he and all who were with him were amazed at the catch of fish that they had taken; and so also were James and John, sons of Zebedee, who were partners with Simon. Then Jesus said to Simon, "Do not be afraid; from now on you will be catching people." When they had brought their boats to shore, they left everything and followed him. —Luke 5:1-11

Many of the unforgettable childhood songs involve hand motions. For instance, the "Itsy Bitsy Spider," "I'm a Little Tea Pot," "Twinkle, Twinkle Little Star." For the evangelical subculture of my generation there was "I will make you fishers of men, fishers of men, fishers of men. I will make you fishers of men if you follow me" and as you sang this, you cast out your imaginary line and reeled it in. Cast it out, reeled it in. I've been disturbed now for nearly twenty-four straight hours by this song, which is running through the back of my mind even now, which began to seem like the oddest thing in the world to put in the mouths of babes.

I'm really not a believer in the need to purge our children's world of every little symbolic suggestion that darkness exists. I think there's a legitimate place in their mythical world for Zurg, Mo Jo Jo Jo, Overcat, bad guys. But I think it might be a good idea not to unconsciously promote a potentially gruesome metaphor without acknowledging a little of its darker qualities. Like, fishing for men. Think of the graphic details. Often the power of a metaphor is precisely in its graphic details. You cast and you hook a fish. It desperately writhes and flips, madly fighting for its life. A fish is never caught without a struggle, not even if you're fly fishing artfully in some remote and serene mountain stream. And for the large majority of sportspeople? It's about piercing the little fishies' flesh with a sharp barb and dragging it to its death.

Imagine that you are fishing for humans. Or, worse, catching humans. Imagine your five-year-old imagining that he is fishing for humans: casting then hooking a kindergarten classmate, dragging him across the shore by the hook implanted in his lips. That's gruesome. The kids probably love it. The boys especially always seem to love anything that suggests fighting or blood or, of course, guts. Maybe little boys everywhere have always been into the fishing for men song in ways their Sunday School teachers would be horrified to learn.

I'm not saying it's a bad song. Maybe it's a great song, with all the thorny potential of a dark folk tale. However, I think it would be good to acknowledge that there's darkness instead of, say, expecting the kids to smile sweetly as they cast and reel and pretend to fish for humans.

It seems like so often, maybe out of familiarity or domestication, these sorts of biblical images slip by us without us even being startled by their force. And I think there's something to be said for being startled. Maybe we are more likely to be jarred from our sleep when we hear in our Bible songs, or in the Bible, some of its unfamiliar harmonies, shifting textures, its profuse teeming plurality of notes, its generative cacophony, its stresses and contradictions and ambiguities instead of just one melody we've come to know and love.

Almost everything you find in the New Testament has some sort of background in the Old Testament, which was of course the Scriptures of the day. And it's often a good place to go to hear a jarring or less familiar note. You'll find fishers of men here. In Jeremiah they are sent out to search every crevice and crack and little pool where the unrepentant little fishies might try to hide. The fishers are to catch and expose them and all their polluted, idolatrous, abominable ways. Amos says God will fish out every last one of those who oppress the poor, who crush the needy, and drag those oppressors away with hooks.

I think it was somewhere around midnight last night that I began to hear that old fishers of men tune but with these new words: "God will drag the oppressors away, the oppressors away, the oppressors away. God will drag the oppressors away, and find them wherever they hide." It's dark, but I thought it was catchy.

Often what people have taken from the text we read tonight in Luke is this simple formula: to be a disciple of Jesus is to be a fisher of men. As if "fishing for humans" was a good *model* for discipleship, some directions we should follow. I think this is pretty clearly not a very good reading of the story. It is extracting a model for discipleship from a very strange metaphor that I doubt was meant to be extracted as a model for discipleship.

There is a certain strain of evangelism that has over-enthusiastically seized upon this metaphor without the irony or ambiguity or complexity (or humor even) which might be appropriate to it. There's a whole history of American revivalism that has a sportsmen feel to it, a macho sort of hunting fishing competitive tone. Billy Sunday takes off his jacket, rolls up his sleeves and prowls the stage, like a hunter, or a fisherman who has honed his skills, his techniques, his expertise and is determined to land an impressive, a big, a huge fish. Maybe that's not some unconditionally horrible song that should never be sung, but I don't hear the Billy Sunday song in this story from Luke.

If there's anything clear in Luke, it's that the mission Jesus embarks upon is one of *release*. Release from the forces that alienate humanity from each other and God and creation, the cages that oppress and separate and bind. So the mission of the followers of Jesus, the disciples, the church will surely have that character of releasing.

Well, fishing is *catching* which seems to be nearly as opposite of *releasing* as you can get.

Where is the release, what is released, is there any release in this passage? Jesus doesn't actually set out to go fishing in the story. What happens is that the people, urgently desiring to hear the word of God (maybe seeking release) press upon him so that he is backed up against the sea. He sees a boat and thinks he'll speak from there. It happens to be Simon's boat. It seems like there's nothing to particularly recommend either Simon or his boat. It and he just happen to be there.

But when Jesus has ceased speaking the Word of God (the word of release, of freedom) to the crowd, Jesus says to Simon: "put out into the deep and let down your nets for a catch." Put out into the deep and let down your nets for a catch.

Now that sounds a provocative note. Remember that in the Bible (and all sorts of ancient literature) the deep is everything that threatens us: *darkness*, death, chaos, uncertainty, and even in completely contemporary use the deep almost always refers to the mysterious, the unknown, what we can't readily see, or don't usually see.

Or how about this interesting variation on the theme: postmodern psychoanalysis refers to our unconscious as a net at the bottom of which a catch of fish will be found. Or this: some contemporary scholars talk about revelation as actually a fishing net which drags the depths of our being, of being itself. At the bottom of the net, they say, a catch of fish will be found.

Simon is fairly certain that there is nothing, no fish, to be caught. As far as he's concerned, he's been fishing a long time and the nets keep coming up empty. But when Jesus speaks, Simon is compelled, in spite of what would normally make sense to him, in spite of what would seem to him to be professionally prudent, to let down his nets into the deep.

The result is really quite traumatic for him, dreamlike, miraculous, or nightmarish. It's hard to distinguish. *There are so many fish*. A lovely delightful lavish abundance? A slithering writhing morass? Beautiful or frightening or both? The text certainly suggests an element of danger. This absurdly fecund, enormous catch of fish threatens to sink the boat. Simon is obviously enormously disturbed by what came up from the depths.

Some commentators on this biblical text read the story very literally and rationally as Luke's attempt to explain plausibly why Simon and the disciples would follow Jesus. It's all very simple to explain. Jesus impressed them by catching a lot of fish. So they left their families and homes, their lives, their careers, everything they ever had, to follow him. Somehow I think it's possible that there was a little more of a crisis involved.

"When Simon Peter *saw* it, he fell down at Jesus's feet, saying depart from me for I am a sinful man." Saw what? A lot of fish? Or maybe, everything he ever feared writhing around in the bottom of the boat? The darkest corners of being brought to light? Mysteries revealed? death? chaos? uncertainty? The depths of who he was, who we are, the depths of humanity, or of being itself? Splayed out all over the boat. This slithering morass up from the depths, and Jesus (God incarnate) sits there on it.

I think it's legitimate to imagine yourself in Simon's place for a moment. Jesus in the same boat as you, next to you, sitting on your fish: what's been hauled up from the absolute darkest scariest place anyone ever imagined, knee deep in sardines, catfish on his lap, traces of the depths (your depths), the smell of fish on his hands. You're both on the verge of being buried by this unbelievably large catch.

Simon seems to have an absolute crisis. I don't know if you can blame him. Jesus has brought all these "fish" up, into the nice little comfortable place they were sitting, into Peter's boat. "Depart from me." That's Peter's response. I think this might be my response: "Please. Leave. This is madness."

But Jesus says, "Don't be afraid." That's his response. He's not afraid. He's not appalled. He's not angry. He anticipates it. He's seen it all before (and before and before), all those "fish": trout and jellyfish and eels and big crabs and sharks and serpents and anything anyone could ever haul up from the deep.

It's a pervasive theme throughout the Bible that everything hidden will be made known. The darkness will all come to light. What is concealed will be revealed. What a startling assertion. It seems like a frightening prospect. *Maybe* unspeakable beauty, but there's all the darkness, the vulnerability, everyone's deepest needs, what we can't face or even name, made known. Who doesn't balk at that, hide from it, deny it?

But maybe the story of Jesus (God incarnate) is that God puts God's self in our boat. God looks at all that and loves us, it, the depths of our being, the depths of being itself. God looks at everything we're afraid of and says "don't be afraid." Perhaps that's why Simon left everything to follow Jesus. Perhaps that's the note that releases us from the forces of alienation and separation, excommunication, estrangement, hate, division, exclusion. Don't be afraid. All manner of darkness may be made known but it doesn't overcome the light.

Sleeping God

June 22, 1996: Fifth Sunday of Pentecost

∽

On that day, when evening had come, he said to them, "Let us go across to the other side." And leaving the crowd behind, they took him with them in the boat, just as he was. Other boats were with him. And a great windstorm arose, and the waves beat into the boat, so that the boat was already being swamped. But he was in the stern, asleep on the cushion; and they woke him and said to him, "Teacher, do you not care that we are perishing?" And he awoke and rebuked the wind, and said to the sea, "Peace! Be still!": And the wind ceased, and there was a great calm. He said to them, "Why are you afraid? Have you still no faith?" And they were filled with awe, and said to one another, "Who then is this, that even wind and sea obey him?" —Mark 4: 35-41

Then the Lord answered Job out of the whirlwind: "Who is this that darkens counsel by words without knowledge? Gird up your loins like a man, I will question you, and you shall declare to me. Where were you when I laid the foundation of the earth? Tell me, if you have understanding. Who determined its measurements—surely you know! Or who stretched the line upon it? On what were its bases sunk, or who laid its cornerstone when the morning stars sang together and all the heavenly beings shouted for joy? Or who shut in the sea with doors, when it burst out from the womb: when I made clouds its garment, and thick darkness its swaddling band, and prescribed bounds for it, and set bars and doors, and said, 'Thus far shall you come, and no farther, and here shall your proud waves be stopped.'?"—Job 38: 1-11

If I'm going to be overwhelmed by the storm, overcome with radical insecurity, anxiety, irrational fear, it will usually happen in the middle of the night. What triggers the attack for me is often a mystery, often mundane. It probably will have something to do with human mortality, but it may be nothing more than the neglected space under the sink that's filling with mildew and mouse turds.

Maybe it's just a sense that my life is spinning out of control or maybe I read an article before going to bed about mutating, drug resistant, micro-organisms passed from chickens to people in China and instead of blissfully being carried away by sleep when I close my eyes, I start doing an extensive mental inventory of who Miles (my two year old) has come into contact with (in, say, the last two years) and if it's possible he had contact with any Chinese chicken farmers.

Often my night anxieties seem to have to do with carcinogens and where carcinogens are concerned, it doesn't take long for me to work up a pretty good anxiety about what we've recklessly done to the environment. And I worry about what's going to happen to our hormones, and our lungs and the world and at 3am, feeling and acting like Woody Allen, I become convinced that I have cancer.

Of course, I don't stop with that—this is just the beginning of a long scary story. I imagine the color of the doctor's office and what her voice will sound like when she says, "Debbie, your tumor is malignant," and how terrible chemotherapy will be, and if I'll shave my head or wear funky hats and maybe I should try alternative medicine instead of chemo, and how frightening to have to face death this way, and will Jim re-marry and who, and I hope so...but not too soon...and I wonder if I know anyone who would be a good mother for Miles and is there any way I can get this all arranged right away. And I'm terribly, terribly, afraid.

Inevitably, Jim, my husband, is oblivious to the storm. Sound asleep. I try sighing loudly, looking at him hard. I whisper, "Jim, are you awake?" He's not. At 3am when you are experiencing the height of human insecurity and angst, a sleeping mate is an acutely painful indication of how utterly alone you really are. It seems that so often the people I love and depend on are sleeping in my greatest hour of need.

This is a funny little story in the gospel of Mark: the disciples face death. The one that is supposed to care for them sleeps. Of course, their storm is real, not the paranoid musings of an insomniac hypochondriac. They have very good evidence—concrete, physical reason to believe their death may be imminent. A lot of them were fishermen, after all. They weren't city boy land lovers scared of a minor squall. They were highly experienced on the sea, and they realized they were going down. This was a bad storm.

In a moment of terror, they scream at their leader who is fast asleep, "Don't you care about us?!" It's actually a little hard for me to imagine. Sleeping seems so indicative of carelessness. How is it even possible when you're on a small sort of boat, obviously not a motor boat, probably a sail boat. I imagine it's tipping pretty far back and forth, heeling, like sail boats do, so that a person would have to hold on if they didn't want to slide right off. And the story says "the waves beat onto the boat." The whole scene had to be very wet, very noisy, very chaotic.

Could Jesus really sleep, rolling back and forth, with water crashing over him? It's an absurd image. When I read this story it doesn't strike me as the "astounding event of the stilling of the sea," but the absurd tale of the God who sleeps, in a storm. Who is this? A Messiah who sleeps through uproarious chaos: not a vigilant warrior (not in this story), but a relaxed sleeper.

"Who then is this?" is the question the disciples ask in the story, and it's not really answered. Mark actually does this a lot in his gospel: asks a lot more questions than he answers. Maybe he thinks that sometimes questions are more important than answers. Maybe because questions prod the reader to respond. Statements cut things off, in a way: they end with a period. If I make a statement, you can listen, and then turn around and leave. But questions sort of require relationship: they require the listener to become engaged, to respond. Maybe Mark writes with questions because living life with God, living life with a living being, is more like asking questions than knowing answers.

"Who is this?" The implications of the question in the gospel story we read, are really pretty important. It implies that people who think they know Jesus, even people who become his disciples, may find themselves realizing that he's unfamiliar.

The reading from Job, paired with the Mark story in the lectionary, has questions with similar implications. God asks Job, "Where were you when I laid the foundation of the earth? Go ahead tell me, if you have understanding..." I think it's a little bit sarcastic. God is asking Job, who are you, that you think you know all the answers? Do you really think you comprehend God? I think its pretty clear we don't and won't ever have it all figured out. But maybe the goal isn't really to arrive at an answer. Maybe the goal is to keep asking questions.

The sea figures prominently in both texts. The sea is the archetypal symbol of the forces that threaten humanity, the abode of chaos, the primeval symbol of death, the cosmic abyss, the dwelling place of the ancient monsters: the eaters and devourers, the place of radical insecurity. The Sea is a nightmare for the anxiety prone, for Woody Allen, the dread of the insomniac.

In almost all the ancient myths the gods do battle with the sea, violently conquering the great sea monsters. There's a little of that kind of thing going on here, but what's remarkable to me is that (in both texts actually) it's not set up like the force of the sea and the force of God are arch enemies. The passage in Job says that God keeps the sea in check (shuts the sea in with doors).

The imagery the writer uses is almost as if the sea were God's child. The passage says "the sea bursts forth from the womb," and "God makes clouds its garment and thick darkness its swaddling band." You swaddle babies. It's almost like God's dressing this little new born child.

The text says God prescribes bounds for the sea and says "thus far shall you come, and no farther." It sounds almost parental: You can play in the yard...but don't cross the line. It doesn't quite sound like the sea is so very threatening to God, some monstrous reality on the verge of devouring God. It doesn't even sound that much like an enemy.

So often what is brought out about the story in Mark is that Jesus is the victor in the struggle with chaos. He stills the storm. And that does seem to be what impresses the disciples. It impresses me. It's so much what I want. Chaos defeated. But perhaps Jesus sleeping through the storm indicates that he's a lot more relaxed about this so called enemy than we are.

Perhaps we think we have a pretty clear idea about the enemy, what is really a threat. Perhaps we expect the gospel to exhort us to be ever alert against this threat, or to promise us rescue. Perhaps we expect Jesus to conform to the archetypal symbol of the vigilant warrior taming the beast. I don't think we would necessarily expect this story about a relaxed guy snoring amidst the chaos. Who is this?

I read in the commentaries that the miracle here is clearly the rescue of the disciples from chaos, but I wonder if the really miraculous, incomprehensible, mysterious, marvelous miracle, is that Jesus slept through the storm. Even this frightening thing, this archetypal chasm, filled with all humanity's fears and insecurities and uncertainties...did not disturb him. He slept through its raging.

Maybe Jesus sleeping in the storm gives us a glimpse of what faith looks like. Maybe sometimes it looks more like sleeping than vigilance: an incredibly peaceful certainty that God will provide your every need, a way of being so completely unthreatened, totally secure, complete faith in God as creator and sustainer of all, utter confidence that God will make things right. Maybe faith could mean a relaxation so profound that one could sleep through the storm.

Perhaps this is the faith that the disciples lack in the boat in the storm. In this particular story it doesn't seem like they primarily lack faith in Jesus's ability to do something about the storm. It seems like they expect that he will. That's why they wake him up, after all. They're saying "Wake up! Do something!" Maybe Jesus asks, "Do you have no faith?" because they didn't share his sleep.

Maybe it's not so much like: What? You have no faith? You think I'd let you sink to the bottom of the sea? Of course I'm going to fix this, you faithless people. But more like: What? You have no faith? You think if the storm tips you over and you sink to the bottom I'm not there? You think you have anything to fear? You think if you drowned, I wouldn't hold you all the way down?

In the Job passage God speaks out of the whirlwind, the chaos, the deep. God claims to have walked in the deepest darkest depths of the sea. Perhaps Jesus can sleep through the raging storm because he's used to moving in the chaos. Maybe he can sleep through the storm because he's used to waves engulfing him. He's no stranger to the depths. Drowning's no threat.

If God's ultimate enemy is chaos, then, I don't know, it seems to me God's losing the battle. I have a two year old. Every time I stack one block on top of another, he knocks it down. I arrange food neatly on his plate: he chews it up, spits it out, flings it on the floor. Chaos defines my life. It seems to define the world.

We control so little. And our fervid attempts to manage may sometimes help people but often wreck everything. I believe in organizing. I guess you can't live without trying, but it seems like you can't keep the mess at bay forever or even for long. This seems true whether you are organizing labor unions or for an end to poverty, whether you are trying to manage the forest or the Persian Gulf. Some messes may be ugly and deadly (there may be unforseen side effects, there may be drug resistant viruses) others may be beautiful and creative, but I'm afraid if Jesus doesn't go down into the primordial chaos, he's never going to reach us. This universe. I don't really think that the faith Jesus witnesses to as he sleeps, on the boat, in the storm, is the faith that we'll all always be rescued from the chaos, the uncertainty, the deep. I think it reaches deeper, if you will, reaches the deep.

I think the hope that faith promises is that your boat could shatter in a million pieces, and it would be okay. You could drown in the storm, and it would be okay. There's no place you can go, no thing you can be, nothing that can happen, that is beyond God's reach.

If Jesus came to me in the middle of my insomniac, hypochondriac anxiety and asked: "Why are you afraid? Have you no faith?" I'd have to answer, "Well, I guess not, I'm not sleeping, I can't sleep. I'm afraid of the storm. I'm afraid my boat's gonna break in a million pieces. I'm afraid to drown."

Part of what's so hopeful to me about this passage is that Jesus doesn't bat the disciples on the head for being afraid, doesn't abandon them for being faithless cowards. Rather, he stills the storm. Maybe he knows it's not really a threat, but he's not too proud to make this concession to their fear, to reach them in this way on this day.

But I think the faith that lets Jesus sleep, must be really, profoundly, deeply, hopeful: a faith not confined to shallow water and a quiet breeze, but one that extends through every storm, to every boat that has ever capsized, every sailor that ever sunk, to the bottom of the sea.

I think the faith that lets Jesus sleep is a faith that God reaches very far for us: if our boat's wrecked, if we're drowning, if, like the disciples, we have no faith. The story doesn't point to a requirement (some stipulation) that I learn to sleep in the storm, while the boat rolls me back and forth, while the water pounds against me. That's crazy. I could never do it.

But, the story is about Jesus sleeping. The story points me, in my sleeplessness, not to meditation techniques or tapes of ocean sounds, not to some threat that if I don't relax, I'll be lost. The story points me instead to Jesus, whose sleeping witnesses to a promise, to a God who reaches beyond what I can even comprehend to be with us. It points to a God who becomes a vulnerable baby, dies a painful death, walks in the deep, calms the storm, reaches far, reaches deep, not necessarily to lift us out, but to walk with us there. I hope, however much faith we lack, we can somehow, some way, go in peace, knowing God is with us.

God Gets Wet

July 20, 1997: Tenth Sunday of Pentecost

∽

Immediately he made his disciples get into the boat and go ahead to the other side, to Bethsaida, while he dismissed the crowd. And after saying farewell to them, he went up on the mountain to pray. And when evening came, the boat was out on the sea, and he was alone on the land. When he saw that they were straining at the oars against an adverse wind, he came toward them early in the morning, walking on the sea. He intended to pass by them, but when they saw him walking on the sea they thought it was a ghost, and cried out; for they all saw him, and were terrified. But immediately he spoke to them and said, "Take heart, it is I; don't be afraid." And he got into the boat with them and the wind ceased. And they were utterly astounded, for they did not understand about the loaves, but their hearts were hardened.—Mark 6:45-52*

I've been a minister at a Christian church now for several years and still I find it a little bit embarrassing outside of the context of a sermon to talk much about Jesus. It's one thing to talk about God. Nobody really cringes when you talk about "spirit" and "soul." But, Jesus, flesh and blood? It makes people uncomfortable.

Obviously there wouldn't have been Christianity without Christ nevertheless the whole thing would seem a lot more plausible, if you could keep it all a little more abstract, and general. Jesus is so specific. It's so unrealistic. It's almost offensive.

And Jesus walking on the water? Not only is that unlikely, but I personally would not describe it as awesome. It's somehow smaller than awesome and it's weird. Not Cirque Du Soleil but the County Fair. A few flashing lights, not-very-fresh cotton candy and a seedy trailer with garish lettering on the side: "Cow with two heads! Lizard Boy! Man walks on water! See it all! One dollar!"

The story is just more odd than it is impressive. A quirky sideshow, not a grand stand event. There's something impotent about it. Jesus *walks* on the water. He doesn't fly like super man. He doesn't zoom, dash, or soar. It's not straight forward heroism. When I read this story I don't feel the same unambiguous admiration for Jesus as I do for Jean Luc Piccard when he rescues the Enterprise with such nobility and good looks. I don't immediately recognize Jesus as a savior.

Maybe some of that lack of recognition has to do with the fact that I live near the end of the twentieth century. Rockets to the moon are *passé*. Science is impressive *and* realistic. Who in the twentieth century cares or knows what to make of a guy walking on water? But the book of Mark actually makes it abundantly clear that people in the first century also had trouble recognizing Jesus.

In this story he actually sort of freaks out the disciples. When they see Jesus walking on the water, their first response isn't: "Wow. Cool. God." They're terrified by him. The text says: "they thought it was a ghost, and cried out." One manuscript even translates this as "demon." They clearly don't recognize him as a savior.

I have a distinct memory of the flannel board version of this story, and Jesus-the-flannel-board-figure walking on the water looked very nice and noble and maybe a little handsome, certainly not scary, and quite dry.

Somehow, even though he was on the water and the wind was blowing and the waves were crashing all around.

In fact he was so easy to recognize in the white robe, with the long brown hair, that the impression I had as a kid was that the guys in the boat were *bad* not to recognize him, and wimpy to be afraid. I think the general feeling in the Sunday School was that if we were on the boat, we would have applauded at the sight of Jesus. Or shouted reverent greetings.

But now, I think that not recognizing Jesus is probably an almost universal response. And maybe it's an appropriate response. If God is alive and if Jesus reveals who God is and if a revelation is something you didn't already know being made known to you, then Jesus maybe would be a little bit unfamiliar every time you encounter him. Maybe we're just meeting a figment of our own or some Sunday School teacher's imagination if Jesus doesn't strike us as a little odd.

Throughout Mark, the disciples (the people who chose Jesus) understand little or nothing of what his actions imply. The incomprehension is so thorough that some people have suggested it must be a Markan device to flatter the reader. We, the readers, are in the know, and can jeer at the characters for being so obtuse. But honestly, most of the time, I feel more obtuse than in the know.

People's incomprehension and lack of recognition doesn't seem to hinder Jesus that much. In this story Jesus makes his way to a boat full of people who can't recognize him, a boat full of people who think he's a ghost or a demon. A boat full of confused people making headway painfully, against the wind. Somehow, that seems like a pretty good metaphor for what it's like to be human.

We don't seem to make that much progress. We're surrounded by enormous human ingenuity and at the same time such unmitigated havoc. We develop antibiotics, but then we end up with super viruses. We develop technology to free us, that ends up enslaving us. We're poisoning our waters. The globe is warming. No matter what we do, how we plan, children die, our parents die.

The wind can be frightening. You can attempt to insulate yourself with insurance policies and water filters, with as much order as you can muster or as much busyness as you can create. You can cover yourself from head to toe in Goretex but when the wind catches you naked, and when the waves are lapping over the side of the boat, you'll get wet.

Water, in the world of Hebrew symbolism, meant chaos. It's an important theme in Mark (and all over the Bible). Mark actually skips the birth narrative of Jesus, the whole childhood, and starts his story with Jesus immediately being baptized. Mark begins his story about God incarnate, with God getting wet.

In the story we read today, Jesus starts out alone, dry, on the land, up on a mountain. Praying. Peaceful. He sees the disciples struggling in the wind and he joins them down in the sea: the anomie, the chaos. He gets his feet wet. He gets his robe wet. I bet he gets soaked.

There's something a little disconcerting about a God who doesn't stay dry. I might recognize God on the mountain before I'd recognize this Man/God getting blown and jostled and wet. Maybe we'd all have a little easier time recognizing Jesus if he would have stayed up on the mountain and cleared everything up from there. If he just would have obliterated every trace of every wind, every storm, all the chaos, from the beginning. But when this scraggley dripping wet figure makes an appearance, it's just not what you expect from a savior. It feels unfamiliar.

When Jesus sees the disciples in the boat struggling against the wind, he waits until the fourth watch of the night, and then (the text says), he "means to pass them by." That seems rude: he means to pass them by. You'd think it would say, "he meant to rescue them or stop the wind or take all the pain out of the world." In Exodus, Moses asks God to show him God's glory and God says, "You can't see my face and live, but I will pass by you. There's a place by me where you can stand upon the rock, and while my glory passes by I will put you in a cleft of the rock and I will cover you with my hand until I have passed by you."

A little earlier in Mark's narrative, Jesus is in the boat with the disciples, in another raging wind, and the boat's filling with water and everyone's terrified, and he's sleeping. It makes him seem a little cool, maybe callous, certainly odd. But he ends up responding to the disciples' fear with compassion in both stories.

Perhaps his "passing by" and his "sleeping" are less an indication of indifference than relaxation. He's relaxed about the wind, the water beating into the boat, the chaos, in a way that is difficult to comprehend: he can sleep through it. He strolls on it. The wind can seem so infinite and so frightening. When you're in it, it seems like it will never stop. Maybe Jesus is free to sleep, to pass them by, because he knows the wind is finite.

Nevertheless, the people in the boat are terrified. They don't perceive. They don't see what he sees. They don't know what he knows. The story indicates that their experience in the wind might have been altered if they had understood "about the loaves." Right before the walking on the water story comes the story of the feeding of the five thousand, where this multitude is fed from five loaves and two fish. Apparently some of the confusion and the fear, the lack of recognition on that boat in the water had to do with the disciples "not understanding about the loaves."

"About the loaves" becomes this mysterious phrase that seems like the key to it all. Like if only we understood "about the loaves," maybe we'd have faith, not be afraid, know everything or something. What about the loaves? Jesus isn't trying to impress the crowd in that story with a magic multiplication of loaves and fishes. Actually the crowd isn't even aware of what's going on. Jesus does it for the disciples. They are anxious about people getting fed. They think everybody should be sent away to find their own food. They were worried because by all appearances, the crowd would go hungry. As it turns out, everyone gets fed.

What at first seemed meager to the disciples (five loaves and two fish) turns out to be unlimited, ample, abundant. I love the story of the feeding of the multitude. It's huge to me because it points to some unfathomably huge grace. Really unfathomable. Unfamiliar. Unexpected. Bigger and different than anyone thought possible. Nurturing, yet strange. It all points to the unfamiliar activity of a God who promises to provide for us, feed us, but who nevertheless doesn't obliterate all our suffering, rather meets us there in the wind. A God who says, I am the bread of life and a God who gets wet. Everyone gets wet. Everyone gets fed.

The disciples didn't understand about the loaves. So when Jesus gets in the boat, and calms the storm, they are utterly astounded. If they had understood that everyone would be fed, maybe they would have been relaxed about the wind, and they wouldn't have been surprised when the wind ceased. Everywhere in the book of Mark, people are said to be in awe, amazed, surprised, astonished beyond measure, and overcome with amazement. But I think we often read "they didn't understand about the loaves" and assume we do understand about the loaves.

Well, if my sometimes overwhelming sense of terror in the wind is any indictation of my understanding, then I think I've often assumed wrongly. I'm anxious about the sufficiency of the bread. I think it's all just way too wet and it's never going to dry out and the mold will probably grow and grow and consume the entire world. The wind is so relentless that no one is ever going to get anywhere. The forces against us are too big. Capitalism has consumed our souls. The profit motive is victor. Whatever we do, however we act, we'll cause some neurosis in our kids, like our parents did in us. It's endless.

Amidst this, it's a little odd, a little surprising, to hear the words: "Take heart, it is I, don't be afraid." Who's "I" and what evidence is there that we shouldn't be afraid? Paul says that "the whole creation is subject to futility in hope." That's a shocking thing to say. It's a revelation.

Do I understand about the loaves? I mean I know what I learned in Sunday School, and I know quite a bit about theology and I've read a lot of commentaries, but do I understand "about the loaves?" I mean, really understand—do I comprehend: bodily, emotionally, soulfully?

We're soaked. We're hungry. But the wind will cease and everyone will be fed. This is unfamiliar, this hope. It is astounding. It is so unfamiliar that it's incredibly difficult to articulate. I don't know that it can be comprehended. I think it's pointed to by these strange stories in the Bible: Jesus walking on the water, a God who becomes human, who dies on the cross, for our salvation, a God who suffers and dies and gets wet.

But I don't think it matters if you read your Bible every day, or spend your whole life in church, when Jesus, when the Word, comes it will rattle you somehow, maybe even astound you. I think we're quite a bit like the confused disciples in the boat, making headway painfully, believing the wind is infinite, believing that everybody better get their own food, believing that everybody better be as heavily insured as possible, better keep themselves thoroughly covered: achieve maximum protection from the water. Don't ever be caught naked. Most the time we're rowing like crazy against the wind, trying to outrun chaos or something, but Jesus walks on the water.

If we see him out there it might shock us. I don't think it's easy to recognize him, but the hope isn't dependent upon our ability to comprehend it. Jesus recognizes us. He goes right ahead and gets in the boat with the dense and the uncomprehending disciples, and the wind does cease. Take heart, he says, I know you don't quite believe it but the bread is sufficient.

Dog Woman

August 18, 2002: Thirteenth Sunday of Pentecost

Jesus left that place and went away to the district of Tyre and Sidon. Just then a Canaanite woman from that region came out and started shouting, "Have mercy on me, Lord, Son of David; my daughter is tormented by a demon." But he did not answer her at all. And his disciples came and urged him, saying, "Send her away, for she keeps shouting after us." He answered, "I was sent only to the lost sheep of the house of Israel." But she came and knelt before him, saying, "Lord, help me." He answered, "It is not fair to take the children's food and throw it to the dogs." She said, "Yes, Lord, yet even the dogs eat the crumbs that fall from their masters' table." Then Jesus answered her, "Woman, great is your faith! Let it be done for you as you wish." And her daughter was healed instantly.—Matthew 15: 21-28

I sometimes think it's just amazing we don't go really way crazier living within the fabrications that structure our world. And how does all that false structure ever manage to contain the chaos that it so misrepresents? Or maybe we're really already just so crazy we don't even notice it anymore. We see but we don't perceive, hear but don't understand (and all that). We just turn right, turn left, stop, go, wear this, eat here, watch that and we're really all insane, blind to some truth or some chaos swirling all around us. But we look pretty normal.

You should see *The Cruise*. It's a documentary about Timothy "Speed" Levitch, a completely not normal seeming guy, who's a double-decker tour bus guide in Manhattan. There's a great scene where he's recalling a conversation he had with one of his tourists. He'd been talking to her about "the grid plan," the layout of avenues and streets in square blocks all over Manhattan. Talking about how the grid plan emanates from a lie and how he'd really like to blow it up and rewrite the streets to be (as he puts it): "much more a self portraiture of our personal struggles rather than some real estate broker's wet dream from 1807."

Apparently the tourist is a little taken aback. She says "I never even thought of that. I can't even imagine that. Everyone likes the grid plan. How could you not like the grid plan? It's so functional. Everyone likes the grid plan."

As he's recalling this conversation in the film Levitch is really agitated. "Who's everyone?" he says. And he stops and the camera stops on someone curled up under a blanket in an alley. "Whoever that is under the white comforter cuddled up with 34th street and Broadway existing on the concrete of this city, hungry and disheveled, struggling to crawl their way through existence, what do they think of the grid plan?" He can't believe that the tourist has never questioned the grid plan.

"What is this woman thinking?" he says, "We're forced to walk at these right angles. I mean, doesn't she find that infuriating? By being so completely allegiant to the grid plan she's like aligning herself totally with this civilization.

"I think most noteworthy is this idiom 'I can't even imagine altering the grid plan.' I can't imagine anything different than this civilization, this lying reality that rules our lives. It's like saying I can't imagine standing up on a chair in the middle of the room to change perspective. I can't imagine changing my mind about anything. Take a right turn, a right turn, a right turn, then there's a red light. And a green light. And a yellow light."

He goes on for maybe ten more minutes about it. I mean yeah, the guy's a little crazy. He rides a double decker bus all over "the grid plan," all over the streets of Manhattan all day, and yet he refuses to give his allegiance to it. He refuses to believe in it. He may live within the structure, but he's still not buying it totally and he's out there to get all the other people riding on the bus to not buy it or believe in it either.

The structures, the grid, the rules of twenty-first century American society are different, obviously, than the structures of first century Palestine. Different enough that it makes it pretty difficult for us to even understand anything in the text at all sometimes. This story about Jesus and the Canaanite woman, is a weird one that way.

In the Biblical world, honor was a huge thing, an elaborate system that structured society, sort of like social status, or class privilege. Some groups of people had more honor by privilege of birth and lineage than others. But unlike social status in our society, honor wasn't a ladder you could climb up. Instead there was a limited amount allotted to you and basically you just had to preserve what you had, make sure you didn't lose any for your group or your clan.

It was what you would call "a limited good society." There was a finite amount of good in the world, a finite amount of honor allotted to you and your family or group. So you had to be really careful about letting any of it go. There's no excess to go around. Public conversations were like little games: honor contests with lots of elaborate rules. On-lookers were all gauging how well the contestants were preserving their relative honor. This story is one of those public encounters.

This encounter is a little off the grid. The scaffolding is not quite holding. It looks a little not normal, a little crazy. Because women aren't really even supposed to play the game at all. The onlookers were probably not guaging, but sucking in their breath. "Oh. My. Gosh. Woman. Get back home woman." She's really risking losing honor by even being out trying to talk to a strange man. And Jesus, by merely speaking to a woman instead of her male representative, is risking honor loss big time. When you think of that, and think of how many times Jesus actually does encounter women in the gospel stories, it's amazing. Crazy.

And then there's this whole thing: Matthew calls her a Canaanite woman. That Matthew chooses to call her that is pretty much like a siren going off. Canaanite is sort of an old fashioned term by Matthew's day, seeing as Canaan hadn't been around for centuries. It was what Israel used to be called before the Israelites slaughtered the Canaanites and took all their land.

In the book of Deuteronomy, the Israelites get instructions as they are going about conquering the land, to kill all the men when they attack a city, but to keep the women and children and animals for their use. *But if it's a Canaanite city?* "You shall save alive nothing that breathes, but you shall utterly destroy them." This is not only a woman that Jesus encounters, but the archetypal enemy of his people.

You would not expect this woman to be here asking this man for healing for her daughter, not in a zillion years. Why is she? It's utterly remarkable crazy wild that the Canaanite woman would want or expect anything at all from the lord of her enemies. It all looks so recklessly inconsiderate of reality. Inconsiderate of normality. In violation of the caution you would expect in the game. A little outside the rules. What about the honor? Isn't she worried?

Isn't he worried? She just calls out, "Have mercy on me, Lord, my daughter is severely possessed by a demon. Help. Save my daughter." The disciples are worried. They're like, "Hey don't threaten the honor, man. Get her away." They're worried. They're guarding it, "It's our bread, man, don't play around with it."

But Jesus speaks to her. That's really something. But he does sort of give her the party line, "I was sent only to the lost sheep of the house of Israel, my people." Then he asks, "Is it fair to take the children's bread and throw it to the dogs?" At that point, I'm pretty sure I'd be like "well, screw you." Or maybe like, "Oh yeah, what was I thinking. I must have lost my head for a moment. Oh yeah, the limited good. Oh yeah, the grid. Oh yeah, I guess I forgot for a moment how things operate, how the world works. Oh yeah, the right angles. And the right angles. And the squares. And the stoplights. Oh yeah, my enemy. Forget I ever asked. Bye."

But she's just not going back there. She's not giving her allegiance to the grid. She may be crazy, but she's just not going to believe in the limitations. She's not going to turn the corner and obey the stoplight. And she knows Jesus is with her. She says, "I'm not asking for the children's bread," as if there isn't enough to go around, enough for everybody, enough for the pets under the table, "the mere crumbs that fall from that plenteous, lavishly graceful bread will be enough." Apparently she's not buying the "limited good society." She's not worried about the scarcity of food, of good, of honor, love, mercy, healing. She may be crazy, but she believes in the unlimited grace of God.

Jesus immediately responds, "Woman, your faith is great." Jesus and the Canaanite woman seem to have an understanding, a hidden alliance, a pact to resist together the structure imposed by a limited good society, the grid that emanates from lies. A pact to resist the notion that "there's not enough." The woman has faith in God, believes that the grace of God can't be contained.

This story is sandwiched between the two stories of the miraculous feedings of the multitudes. In those stories it seems like there's just a little bit of food. And the disciples, of course, are worried that there's a serious scarcity. But as it turns out, over against every apparent possibility, the food is plentiful, lavish, nobody goes hungry. The crumbs are falling all over and they're feeding the multitudes.

There's enough for the Canaanites, unbelievably. Enough for lost sheep, lost goats, gentiles, the lame, Romans even. Enemies, of all varieties. Your enemies, my enemies. There's enough for the pets under the table. Enough for the dogs: for Flippy and Scruffy and Caesar and Iggy and Fender. And probably the cats, too.

However the structures conspire to contain it, the love, grace, mercy of God can't be contained. Not by the walls of first century Jewish religion or the walls of a sexist society or a limited good society, or the grid plan. The realities of the empire can't contain it. Our theology, your brain, even your imagination can't contain it. The mercy and the grace and the love, the food, is not finite. It's infinite, uncontainable, bigger than anything. Damn, that's hard to believe. This woman seems to believe it. At least in this moment.

So. You have to ride the bus, play the games, make money, buy insurance, watch TV. Okay. But you don't have to give your allegiance to it. You don't have to believe in it. It makes a difference where you put your faith. It might confuse and disrupt traffic flow if you don't give your alligance to the grid. It might muck up the clarity that is after all, a lie. It might throw a kink into the system if you believe in God.

How Many Times Should I Forgive George Bush?

September 15, 2002: Seventeenth Sunday of Pentecost

～

Then Peter came and said to him, "Lord, if another member of the church sins against me, how often should I forgive? As many as seven times?" Jesus said to him, "Not seven times, but, I tell you, seventy-seven times. For this reason the kingdom of heaven may be compared to a king who wished to settle accounts with his slaves. When he began the reckoning, one who owed him ten thousand talents was brought to him; and, as he could not pay, his lord ordered him to be sold, together with his wife and children and all his possessions, and payment to be made. So the slave fell on his knees before him, saying, 'Have patience with me, and I will pay you everything.' And out of pity for him, the lord of that slave released him and forgave him the debt. But that same slave, as he went out, came upon one of his fellow slaves who owed him a hundred denarii; and seizing him by the throat, he said, 'Pay what you owe.' Then his fellow slave fell down and pleaded with him, 'Have patience with me, and I will pay you.' But he refused; then he went and threw him into prison until he would pay the debt. When his fellow slaves saw what had happened, they were greatly distressed, and they went and reported to their lord all that had taken place. Then his lord summoned him and said to him, 'You wicked slave! I forgave you all that debt because you pleaded with me. Should you not have had mercy on your fellow slave, as I had mercy on you?' And in anger his lord handed him over to be tortured until he would pay his entire debt. So my heavenly Father will also do to every one of you, if you do not forgive your brother or sister from your heart."—Matthew 18:21-35

How often shall my brother or sister or spouse or co-worker, or some stranger or enemy sin against me and I forgive him or her or them? How often shall I be confronted with the unloving, unmerciful occasionally very ugly world, and yet love it, forgive it, its inadequacy and failure. And not just love and forgive the world in some general way, which is not always so hard, but what about George Bush, what about all the people who seem to you to be so evidently tyrannical or brutish or cruel? Or what about the teenager who drove head on into my car, or what about those people who don't just hurt you once but whose failure and limits and irritating habits you have to live with daily? How many times should you forgive them? How deeply? How many people do you have to forgive, anyway?

Peter asks Jesus this question and Jesus makes a little fun of his number thing. "Not seven times. Seventy times seven. Peter, you're counting? Don't count. You can't count. Mercy is not counting. It's beyond calculation, the absence of calculation. You can't keep track of it. It won't fit in your books. Mercy isn't numbers and equations and counting."

Then Jesus says, "The kingdom of God is like..." And you expect him to finish that statement with something like, not at all mathy or numerical. You'd expect him to say the kingdom of God is like "the most outside jazz there ever was. It's like Ornette Coleman, Sun Ra, or it's like Dostoevsky. It's like gorgeous, brilliant, complex, dissonance, outside of math sort of thing."

But actually, strangely, he doesn't say that. He says it's like "a king who wished to settle accounts." Which seems like an unlikely place to start a story that's supposed to illumine a mercy that is way outside of accounting.

How odd really that he even calls it the "king" dom of God. That sort of taints it, doesn't it? "King" dom. I know you might have some good, warm mythic feelings about kings. Everybody likes castles and crowns and princess clothes, but the king thing is really mostly about big money and power and hierarchy and domination and excess and gluttony.

Like King Louis XVI who had ten servants whose sole purpose in life was to groom and dress him. It took ten servants three hours to get him dressed and do his hair. Look at some of the old paintings of royalty sometime. Their hairstyles were five feet high. The servants had to get up on ladders to get that last little bit on top to stand up just right.

And when they were finally finished adorning the king and powdering him and briefing him on the sort of attitude his voice should convey, they had to carry him to his throne because authentic movement was impossible. He was so constructed.

But okay, Jesus wasn't talking about Louis XVI. In first century Palestine, royalty meant the Roman emperors. They were great. Nero had his mother killed to please the woman he was having an affair with, whom he ended up marrying and later killed by kicking her when she was pregnant. Yeah, kings are great.

Some of the emperors were not so sick but they were always all about power and wealth and status. The world of kings is dark, almost by definition.

We need to believe (for some reason) in the kindly benevolent king, Arthur or Babar, all for the people. But you just can't sit on a throne, have all the power, all the money, and be all for the people. I just think power works differently than that. So, the kingdom of heaven is like this king, right, who after spending four hours getting his gold laced tights on and his hair fixed, after kicking his servants, and depriving the peasants of food, wished to "settle accounts," in other words "get a bunch of money": collect the taxes that he's been using to fund the lifestyle of the gluttonous elite at the expense of the unfortunate peasant.

The kingdom of God is like a king? Who was amassing his wealth? What in this story is possibly like God?

A servant is brought in, so the story goes. This is not the demure little guy who wipes the king's chin after breakfast. This servant obviously handles large sums of money, probably collects from the people who collect the taxes. He doesn't sit on the throne all day, but he has some power. In fact his muscles are probably a little more toned than the king's. He's more sporty, he gets out more, likes to ride the horses, probably resents the king (who wouldn't?) for his bloated privilege gained by no virtue of his own but merely the circumstances of his birth, may even be plotting rebellion, who knows. We'll call him Richard.

Richard is brought up before the king and the king peruses his accounting books figuring things out (and here's where the story gets all bendy and out of bounds and surreal). The king looks up and says with a totally straight face: "Oh, Richard, you owe seventy-five billion trillion zillion dollars, actually you owe infinity, you owe...more than everything." And then somebody starts barking like a dog, and a chicken wanders through (not really, but the scene is that surreal).

Richard stands there with his eyes bulging and his mouth hanging open, and the king looks back down at his book, big feather pen in his hand, strikes a big black line through his name, "Richard: Owes *everything*. To be sold with his wife and children and all that he owns." Well, what can Richard do but fall on his knees. There's nothing else to do, no place else to go. So he pleads, "King, have patience with me. I'll repay you."

Well that's kind of ridiculous. Repay infinity? Repay more than every-thing? Repay seventy-five billion trillion zillion dollars? There's no way. So then (taking the surreal quality up yet another notch), the king shrugs, waves his hand, says: "Okay. You're free. You don't owe me a thing. Go on. I release you entirely."

It's like this outlandish shocking thing moves in for a moment, and takes everybody by surprise: the greedy pompous old king, unreliable plotting Richard, anybody listening to the story. In this crazy moment, the mercy moves in. The servant is set free. The accounting is abandoned. The meas-uring stick is thrown out. Infinite forgiveness takes over, and this is what the kingdom of God is like.

When the mercy moves in it's extremely disorienting. The ground upon which you and everything and everybody usually stands is taken out from under your feet. What you know and count on? Whoosh. Like that. Gone. Swept away. And there's unlimited mercy and infinite love in its place. Suddenly it's not about counting (or judging or what anybody owes). The servant, beyond reason, is not held accountable for his failure (and failure and failure again) but is released from it. The mercy moves in. You glimpse it. It shocks you. And then, what happens to it?

You'd think Richard would be flying. You'd think his freedom would set him free, that he'd whistle and wave and skip down the street with a smile. You think he'd hug the first passerby. Call out to all the people on the street, "Hey everybody, did you notice that the earth just moved? I have been released, you have been released, we've all been released. We live in the mercy, man. I love you!"

It's the most impossible thing that instead of that, far from flying, he walks heavily on the ground (that by the way is not really even there). And he seizes the first person he sees by the throat. As if the mercy never happened, precisely as if he still owed the debt, had never been released, and now has to make somebody else pay because he owes a huge debt for his failure.

But he doesn't. It seems impossible that instead of freely breathing that unbelievable, merciful air, he puts his hands around some other guy's throat and chokes him, some little guy who doesn't even have five dollars to pay his debt. And Richard's like, "Pay what you owe. You owe. Look at you. You don't even know that your shoes are totally outdated and your hair looks horrible. And you're stupid and ugly and that was a dumb thing to say. And you're lazy and never do what you say you're going to do. And you're just weak and bad. Pay up loser."

As if it really was all about paying up what you owe and about counting. As if accounting was the biggest truth, though five minutes earlier that ground had been swept away. He acts as if he had never been freed, as if the judgment was the ground of his being, not the mercy.

And this little guy falls down on his knees and he says, "Have patience with me. I'll get better. I'll get stronger. I'll pay you what I owe." But Richard looks at him with disgust, "You ugly, sniveling, weak, bad, ir-responsible, stupid person, you are not released. I do not release you. You are not righteous. You are not good. I can count and you have failed. I do not free you. I judge you. I condemn you. Go to prison and stay there till you earn your way out, you sinner, loser, failure."

(Hey, maybe it's some little guy he chokes, or *maybe*, like in a dream, it's really *himself* just manifesting as a little guy or maybe it's another guy and himself and everybody. You know you can read these stories so many ways.)

The parable jars you into seeing how sad, how tragic it is that the mercy moves in and yet Richard, and yet the servant, and yet we do not live in the mercy, do not live inside the truth created. And then (it seems almost impossible not to make the next move), the other characters in the story, the fellow servants, they witness this mean merciless behavior, and they think (you think), what a jerk.

How can you not pass judgment on the unforgiving servant? Such an unmerciful, unloving, violent, recalcitrant must be held accountable for his failure. Surely there are grounds for judgment here. Can we bring back in that ground that has been swept away? Surely this is righteousness. This is what the calculus requires, and it like sucks you in and you get all twisted in it. This is the move we always seem to make. We live here. And we don't breathe the mercy. Live by the calculus: be imprisoned by the calculus. We are delivered to the jailers until the last debt is paid.

The parable seems to show that the standards of the world—our standards, what we hold onto like crazy—are totally inadequate for the kingdom (if you can call it that) of God. Who then can be saved? We are given infinite mercy, love, the grace of God. We are created out of it and for it and sustained in it. It is suicidal for us to reject it, to refuse to obey it, to live outside of it. It is murderous to judge when we are not judged, to love only those who love us only when they love us. This is not life lived in the freedom and the love and the mercy of God, but death dealing. This is bombing and hating and war. It isn't freedom but surrender to a false order or disorder, to the calculus which stands outside of the sphere of grace.

I'm afraid this is precisely where we live. Isn't this the world we live in? It seems far from the kingdom of God. Where is infinite love and mercy? No one believes in unlimited mercy. It's unreasonable and unrealistic. It's shocking, maybe dangerous. Everyone lives by the calculus. You don't find mercy in politics, in George Bush's rhetoric, or in the rhetoric of people who hate America. You don't find unlimited mercy and infinite love in the righteousness of the right or in the righteousness of the left. You don't find it in corporate planning or the recording industry or the church.

It's dark. And we are not by any means the light of the world. We very clearly live in the "king" dom of the world. And where does the mercy appear in the world of kings, the world of accounting? Where is the mercy in the calculus? It's not, is it?

But..."the kingdom of God is like a king who wished to settle accounts." Jesus sets his story in the anti-mercy imperial kingdom, the empire, and shockingly, surreally, the mercy moves in, and in one crazy moment, unlimited forgiveness takes over. Shockingly, surreally, God becomes incarnate in this very world. God reached deeply (all the way) into the heart of darkness that we might be freed from it, the counting, the anti-mercy.

We have been released. We need the light to see it, and the light shines in the darkness. The world we live in is the world to which God comes.

A Bomb to the Human Competition Extravaganza

September 19, 1999: Eighteenth Sunday of Pentecost

~

For the kingdom of heaven is like a landowner who went out early in the morning to hire laborers for his vineyard. After agreeing with the laborers for the usual daily wage, he sent them into his vineyard. When he went out about nine o'clock, he saw others standing idle in the marketplace; and he said to them, 'You also go into the vineyard, and I will pay you whatever is right.' So they went. When he went out again about noon and about three o'clock, he did the same. And about five o'clock he went out and found others standing around; and he said to them, 'Why are you standing here idle all day?' They said to him, 'Because no one has hired us.' He said to them, 'You also go into the vineyard.' When evening came, the owner of the vineyard said to his manager, 'Call the laborers and give them their pay, beginning with the last and then going to the first.' When those hired about five o'clock came, each of them received the usual daily wage. Now when the first came, they thought they would receive more; but each of them also received the usual daily wage. And when they received it, they grumbled against the landowner, saying, 'These last worked only one hour, and you have made them equal to us who have borne the burden of the day and the scorching heat.' But he replied to one of them, 'Friend, I am doing you no wrong; did you not agree with me for the usual daily wage? Take what belongs to you and go; I choose to give to this last the same as I give to you. Am I not allowed to do what I choose with what belongs to me? Or are you envious because I am generous?' So the last will be first, and the first will be last.—Matthew 20:1-16

T he first will be last and the last first" is one of the great lines of the Bible. It's like a little bomb Jesus threw out there into the human competition extravaganza. Except nothing exploded. Or at least it doesn't seem like there's been much interruption to the so called rat race. Of course, there's always people who attempt to opt out. But I've seen people climbing all over each other to be the best or most creative, or most relaxed, or spiritually enlightened super alt opter outers.

Or maybe it did explode and one day (or in some moment) the smoke will clear and better brace yourself because, the kingdom of God, God's way, the world according to God, is like a householder who went out early in the morning to hire laborers for his vineyard.

Early in the morning before the sun rose he went out. Who's up so early? The best people are. Admirable kind and hard working people. The Sisters of Mercy are up setting out coffee and rolls for the poor and hungry. There's an earnest little boy up, eager to earn enough money to buy medicine for his sick baby sister. Early in the morning is the symbolic territory of the responsible and the "good." (Why do you think churches meet on Sunday mornings? It's an opportunity to define yourself, situate yourself, among the people of the morning. It's an intentional opposition to Saturday Night.)

The people out there early in the morning, the first, are ready and waiting, eager to work for the householder. They didn't lay in bed repeatedly push-ing the snooze button. In fact they've already been to the gym, toasted their home grown oats for their oatmeal, and sweetened them with honey they collected from their native beehives, which are strengthening eco-logical diversity. They meditated and journaled. They showered, combed their hair, dressed neatly and were ready to work by first light. These are the people who have a good work ethic, (good habits, good intentions, good haircuts). These are people who try hard. They aren't that surprised to be hired, because it's precisely what they've been working toward. But they are pleased—pleased to be hired for a decent wage, pleased to engage in productive work and contribute to society.

And they have several hours of contribution under their belts when the vineyard owner abruptly abandons his managerial position (a little to the dismay of the early workers because although it does not distract them from their work they do notice him noticing them and he can't notice them if he's going back to town for more workers).

When he comes back, his huge extended cab pick up is full of more folks. Folks of the *mid* morning variety. Out looking for work at 9:30? They obviously made an effort, but not a very energetic one. This might indicate a bit of a lack of initiative, a little passivity, maybe the kind of people that, well, sort of let the world happen to them, instead of really working to make a difference. They had cheerios or pop tarts for breakfast on the way out the door and they didn't brush their teeth.

The first people eventually adjust to these latecomers (although in the beginning it's a bit frustrating because they're a little slower), but it doesn't take long for the whole crew to settle into a nice working rhythm. By lunch break there's even a nice comeraderie and everyone's looking forward to sitting down with the owner, maybe getting some feedback on their work performance, hoping to chat with him about the vineyard which was beautiful and full of amazing varietals. But wouldn't you know it, he's off again to town in search of more people.

This time he finds a bunch of people who aren't even looking for work. They crawled out of bed at eleven and were on their way to get a paper (or more like a hot rod magazine or a TV guide) and a donut or a big greasy bacon breakfast. And then they were planning to go back to their couch and watch daytime TV, when this ardent little guy..."hires them."

When he comes back to the vineyard with this load, the first folks understandably feel a little diminished: he so obviously didn't even question their qualifications, or health, or work ethic, or desire, or intentions. And these things seem so vital to them, the first. But they have the expansiveness that comes from a good productive day of work and they recognize that some are less fortunate than themselves and that's probably why these late-comers are prone to crude and off-color jokes, and even though the vineyard owner takes several more trips to town to bring back increasingly less qualified people, the good, kind first folks warm to them and even make plans to invite them over for dinner.

But then it's the last hour of the workday. It's 4:30 in the afternoon. Everything's winding down. And the crazy landowner goes out again, runs into some guy who just woke up, puked, kicked his dog and left his house to start drinking again and...he hires him. Next he spots some pretty rich ladies in sunglasses and furs overloading their poor servants with hat boxes and shoe boxes and gourmet foods and he asks these elegant women: "Why have you been idle all day?" Of course, this amuses them, and they laugh, and lie (with a mixture of condescension, contempt, and ridicule), "Because nobody hired us, darling." And he...hires them.

The householder brings 'em all back, doesn't realize or doesn't care that he's the butt of their jokes, and when the good hard working people see this last bizzare contingent of so-called "workers," pulling in at about 4:55, they are disconcerted.

The giggling ladies in their white gloves and the stinking drunkard have picked about two and a half grapes when the vineyard owner calls them all together, in from the field, to be paid. He pays the last hired a hundred and twelve dollars. A very decent day's wage for a day's work, a ridiculously large wage for people who worked half a second. But he's seemingly oblivious to the fact that the women don't need it and the man will spend it on whiskey. He pays the people who began work at three the same. And the people he hired at twelve and at nine, the same. And the people who have borne the burden of the day and the scorching heat? The earnest little boy saving for his baby sister's medicine, the good and patient mother, the ecologically minded, enviromentally responsible, the Sisters of Mercy, and Mother Thersea, and Jimmy Carter, all the good and earnest and kind people...he pays them one hundred and twelve dollars. Exactly what he paid the last scornful rich lady who lifted one finger for one second.

The first hired are mad. That he even brought in all these people who weren't qualified, who didn't even try, was insulting. That he treated them all the same was intolerable. The owner of the vineyard has indiscriminately, willy nilly, assembled a crew that's in large part unfit, and instead of rewarding the ones who do have some integrity he's treated them all alike.

So. That's what the kingdom of God is like. I'm not sure if this is really the sort of thing people want in their children's Sunday School curriculum. What's the incentive for good behavior? It's not really that edifying. It seems unjust, or at least explodes our calculations about how things ought to be ordered, our definitions of justice: getting what you deserve, equal pay for equal work, paying the consequences of your crime, or reaping the benefits of your labor.

The householder's behavior threatens our definitions, threatens some deep seated understanding we have of how things are or should be. Maybe grace is not exactly always (or maybe hardly ever) quite like a warm soft bunny brushing by. Because it threatens something we rely on and grow up with and learn in school and teach our children: If you do your best you'll be rewarded. You'll be rewarded according to what you achieve. I don't think the first are necessarily disturbed because they are greedy and begrudging, and wanting praise all for themselves. I think they are disturbed because they feel the ground beneath their feet bucking and rocking. The way of the world is being overthrown. Grace is rearranging everything.

We like grace at House of Mercy. We don't even meet early in the morning. We're all for the mercy. But when we come face to face with what we affirm in theory, it's not going to be a bunny in our hands. Maybe a molotov cocktail. It's not like something we're really capable of handling very well. It's all the good people who believe in God's goodness and righteousness and justice who end up killing Jesus, after all. They are mad about the way he's rearranging everything.

Grace, the way of the householder, is a threat. At least from where we stand or at least to the structures and institutions that order our world and to the legal system and pedagogy and the Olympics. It's a threat. The kingdom of God has no merit system. No merit system. No merit system at all. You are not rewarded for your achievement.

This does make you wonder how a righteous God can behave in such a seemingly irresponsible manner. Sometimes people answer the question by saying: well, you have God's mercy on the one hand, which offers forgiveness and love and grace. But then, on the other hand you got God's righteousness which demands justice and someone's blood, which ends up being like punishment and hell. It's as if there were two sides of God, justice and mercy, in opposition to one another. This parable is about mercy. There are other passages about justice and they have a different feel to them.

But by doing that you end up with a God who's a little schizoid, a little Dr. Jekyl/Mr Hyde. Maybe it's just that we don't quite understand justice. The householder seems unjust to us, but maybe our definitions of justice are pale and anemic and narrow and lacking mercy. Maybe God's justice is not in opposition to mercy, but includes it.

Miles, my five year old, drives me crazy lately with his definitions of justice. He's constantly saying "it's not fair." And he's almost inevitably applying it to something to which it doesn't apply. And it's aggravating to have him insist that it's "not fair" that it's getting dark at eight, or that Arthur is on instead of Dragon Tales, or that we're having broccoli for dinner, or that there's no chocolate cookies in the house. I want to yell: "What are you talking about? You are using a word, you are trying to employ a concept, for which you have absolutely no understanding, or it's backwards or please just stop saying 'it's not fair,' you don't know what fair means."

Maybe it's that aggravating for God, or saddening, to watch us employ our definition of justice. Maybe we're that far off. Maybe our categories for justice are unimaginative, more like mathematical calculations: They worked ten hours, they should be paid for ten hours. He stole a million from peasants, he should pay back a million. This is justice, according to our definition. Mercy is something else.

But for God, perhaps, justice is an event, some dramatic and passionate event driven by God's desire to be reunited with us. It's not an abstract equation, it's an event like the cross. It doesn't have to do with some distancing and objective judicial system. It has to do with love and desire and passion.

For us bringing someone to justice means they suffer the consequences of their crime or they are rewarded for their achievements. For God bringing someone to justice means they are brought back into the circle of God's embrace. That's not the opposite of mercy. Justice is to reinstate the connection of the covenant that God has established. It is to restore us in love to each other and God. And maybe the way to get there, at least it seems to be the case in the Bible, in the story of Jesus, is not all sweetness and candy, but that's where God's going in God's justice and in God's mercy.

The householder says he'll give the second and the third and the fourth and the last what is right and what is right turns out to be the same thing for everyone. The "right" is relationship, being embraced by God. It's working in the vineyard with everybody and God. That's the "right." And the householder is shameless in his ardent pursuit to "hire" people, to get them to the vineyard. Who hires thoroughly unfit workers five seconds before the work day is over? It's remarkable, revelational, how urgently the householder seems to need, to want, every last one of the people.

God is shameless and tireless in God's pursuit of us and everybody. God just keeps going back and going back and going back again. And most of the time people aren't even looking to be hired. You don't see grace and justice in this story in the reward, in the wage paid. You see it in the vineyard where everybody, the drunkard, the rich ladies, all the good and bad are gathered together to pick grapes and drink wine.

Food for Worms

March 31, 2002: Fifth Sunday of Lent

~

Now a certain man was ill, Lazarus of Bethany, the village of Mary and her sister Martha. Mary was the one who anointed the Lord with perfume and wiped his feet with her hair; her brother Lazarus was ill. So the sisters sent a message to Jesus, "Lord, he whom you love is ill." But when Jesus heard it, he said, "This illness does not lead to death; rather it is for God's glory, so that the Son of God may be glorified through it." Accordingly, though Jesus loved Martha and her sister and Lazarus, after having heard that Lazarus was ill, he stayed two days longer in the place where he was. Then after this he said to the disciples, "Let us go to Judea again." The disciples said to him, "Rabbi, the Jews were just now trying to stone you, and are you going there again?" Jesus answered, "Are there not twelve hours of daylight? Those who walk during the day do not stumble, because they see the light of this world. But those who walk at night stumble, because the light is not in them." After saying this, he told them, "Our friend Lazarus has fallen asleep, but I am going there to awaken him." The disciples said to him, "Lord, if he has fallen asleep, he will be all right." Jesus, however, had been speaking about his death, but they thought that he was referring merely to sleep. Then Jesus told them plainly, "Lazarus is dead. For your sake I am glad I was not there, so that you may believe. But let us go to him." Thomas, who was called the Twin, said to his fellow disciples, "Let us also go, that we may die with him." When Jesus arrived, he found that Lazarus had already been in the tomb four days. Now Bethany was near Jerusalem, some two miles away, and many of the Jews had come to Martha and Mary to console them about their brother. When Martha heard that Jesus was coming, she went and met him, while Mary stayed at home. Martha said to Jesus, "Lord, if you had been here, my brother would not have died. But even now I know that God will give you whatever you ask of him." Jesus said to her, "Your brother will rise again." Martha said to him, "I know that he will rise again in the resurrection on the last day." Jesus said to her, "I am the resurrection and the life. Those who believe in me, even though they die, will live, and everyone who lives and believes in me will never die. Do you believe this?" She said to him, "Yes, Lord, I believe that you are the Messiah, the Son of God, the one coming into the world." When she had said this, she went back and called her sister Mary, and told her privately, "The Teacher is here and is calling for you." And when she heard it, she got up quickly and went to him. Now Jesus had not yet come to the village, but was still at the place where Martha had met him. The Jews who were with her in the house, consoling her, saw Mary get up quickly and go out. They followed her because they

thought that she was going to the tomb to weep there. When Mary came where Jesus was and saw him, she knelt at his feet and said to him, "Lord, if you had been here, my brother would not have died." When Jesus saw her weeping, and the Jews who came with her also weeping, he was greatly disturbed in spirit and deeply moved. He said, "Where have you laid him?" They said to him, "Lord, come and see." Jesus began to weep. So the Jews said, "See how he loved him!" But some of them said, "Could not he who opened the eyes of the blind man have kept this man from dying?" Then Jesus, again greatly disturbed, came to the tomb. It was a cave, and a stone was lying against it. Jesus said, "Take away the stone." Martha, the sister of the dead man, said to him, "Lord, already there is a stench because he has been dead four days." Jesus said to her, "Did I not tell you that if you believed, you would see the glory of God?" So they took away the stone. And Jesus looked upward and said, "Father, I thank you for having heard me. I knew that you always hear me, but I have said this for the sake of the crowd standing here, so that they may believe that you sent me." When he had said this, he cried with a loud voice, "Lazarus, come out!" The dead man came out, his hands and feet bound with strips of cloth, and his face wrapped in a cloth. Jesus said to them, "Unbind him, and let him go."—John 11: 1-44.

O n Ash Wednesday the church begins the season of Lent by taking what were once living palm fronds waved happily in the hands of children the previous Easter, setting them on fire, and burning them until they're nothing but a black, gritty dust. The priest or pastor—or whoever—then smears the burned up palm fronds on the congregants' foreheads in the shape of a black cross and says, "Remember: you are dust and to dust you shall return."

Though it didn't seem all that heavy when we were doing it, I've been reflecting (perhaps a little too much) on what a graphic, unnerving ritual the introduction to Lent really is. "Remember you are dust and to dust you shall return." That's not just: remember you're going to die. That's: remember, you are going to decompose and become dirt. You become dirt because your body decays. Worms eat your rotting flesh and then process you through their digestive systems. This is how you return to dust.

Well, that's comforting. That's the kind of thing that sends you home all warm and positive and inspired to really get your life together. Remember, to dust you will return, food for worms. It's in the liturgy.

Most of the time we probably try consciously (or more likely unconsciously) to avoid thinking too much about this. Being perpetually aware that you're going to decompose and become worm food could render you a less productive member of society, useless even, mad. It might make it hard to get dressed in the morning if you greeted your reflection in the mirror always conscious of your destiny, "Good morning, worm food. Are you going to comb your hair, brush your teeth and put on some earrings today, worm food?"

If you hold it in your mind: "you are dust and to dust you shall return," it is hard to walk by the cosmetic counters at department stores and watch people trying on perfume and make up, frantically grooming, and not want to whisper in their silly ears: "My, what fancy worm food you are."

It's not that comfortable or enjoyable to sit in a nice restaurant drinking expensive wine and meticulously prepared food and to be all the while hyper aware, or even vaguely aware, that it will eventually merely be processed in the digestive tracts of maggots.

It is not easy to actively remember you are dust and then live real comfortably within polite societal norms, doing all the normal and trivial and routine things that the social order prescribes. So for the most part I think we probably don't actively "remember."

But some psychologists, anthropologists, a lot of people, have surmised that it actually takes a lot of our psychic energy *not* to think about "it." Repression, denial. We have to expend a lot of energy to not remember our inevitable and basic creaturely vulnerability, that we *will* become weak and die. We end up spending a lot of time doing a lot of stuff to try and keep that at bay, to hide it from ourselves and everybody. We hate it and fear it, but we end up giving death so much power that it becomes our biggest idol, and we live in service to it, trying to prove we are not food for worms.

Food for worms doesn't drive fancy cars. We're not vulnerable. Look at our cities. Look at our productivity. Look what we can build. We're not weak. Look at our bombs. Let's make them huge. We're not going to die. Look at our power. We are big and strong and we're gonna keep on getting bigger and stronger. We're not "creatures." Creatures don't have the power to destroy the world at their fingertips.

In service to death we end up not really paying so much attention to life. We're so busy building and destroying to prove our power, trying to look "big" and invulnerable and "not weak" as much as we possibly can.

To remember we are dust causes us "annihilation anxiety." When I was reading to prepare for this sermon, I saw that phrase, and I thought, "That's what I have: annihilation anxiety." Some say it's the basic human fear that's underneath all fears. It's fear of death, fear that the self will be annihilated, but it ends up coming out all over the place as fear of life. Fear to live as who we are, to live fully as human beings, humanely, awake, aware, sometimes fragile always vulnerable creatures who have bodies and experience zillions of things and die.

We may need to repress our annihilation anxiety to function normally in society, to not feel insane in the mall. But it keeps us at some level from living wholly, fully. It keeps us from accepting, embracing, and loving our humanity, our creatureliness, our fragility. It means refusing our humanity and consequently others' humanity, and whatever reminds us we are creatures who die.

It makes us hate and ostracize what seems weak or broken because that reminds us we die. We worship power because power makes us feel like we're not going to die. We reject any sign of the decaying, vulnerable, weak creatureliness in ourselves and in others, and all of creation because we don't want to die.

It's a weird thing. Our fear of death ends up causing us to give death actually a tremendous amount of power to control our lives. It turns out, I think, that we worship death really, make it our God, our greatest idol, the ultimate, all powerful, absolute and final reality, deity. God. Maybe I've just been reading too much Ernest Becker, but this seems true to me.

The story that is the scripture for tonight is about dethroning that idol, death. Not nervously keeping it at bay, but looking it straight in the face. Not denial of death, but resurrection of the dead. I know it's a crazy story. Crazy to suggest that death is not really the power we imagined, not really the end, not really at the bottom of everything. Crazy to suggest that God is really God after all. Death's not God. God is not death. God is resurrection and life.

It's a wild story about a man, Lazarus, who is sick and dying. Mary and Martha, the man's sisters, love their brother and don't want him to die. So they send for Jesus, who also loves Lazarus. They want him to come to save Lazarus, keep him from dying. But Jesus doesn't come to keep him from dying. It seems he wants to show these people, us, maybe everyone something about death and something about trust in God.

When Jesus finally gets there, it's way too late. Lazarus has already been dead four days. When Martha first greets Jesus, it seems obvious that she's not that happy with the situation. She wanted Jesus to prevent her brother's death. She says, "If you would have been here, my brother wouldn't be dead." Like "where were you, you jerk. You could have saved him. You love us? You abandoned us."

I think if I could design a savior just how I wanted a savior (and this may be due to my basic annihilation anxiety,) I would want a savior to save me, protect me and everyone I love from dying. Actually I can hardly think of anything I'd want out of Jesus more than that. I want no death.

But that's not really the kind of savior Jesus is. It's not what you get with this story, though people in their anxiety often try to construe Christianity that way. As if believing in Jesus is somehow an escape from the sadness, the suffering of death. As if we should not feel so horrible that our brother or our baby or our mother or our dad died. We should rejoice because they are in a better place. Well, in this story Lazarus, the dead brother, is plainly decaying in the tomb. Maybe that's a better place, but it doesn't seem like it to me.

This story goes to lengths to show how dead Lazarus is. Totally dead. The Hebrew people believed, apparently, that a person's life force would hover near their dead body for three days, but on the fourth day it would be gone and the dead person would then be beyond hope. Dead is dead. And Lazarus is dead. Beyond hope.

The story doesn't anesthetize death, make it pretty and clean. It emphasizes its graphic quality. It brings up the smell of death. Martha says, "He has been dead four days by this time there will be an odor." The body is decaying and the rotting flesh smells. Look it in the face. You are dust and to dust you shall return. This is not perfume and make up and denial of death. Sometimes people act like if you believe in Jesus, well then, death loses its sting. But that's not the way this story goes. There is great sadness at this death, mourning and weeping. They taste death. They smell it. They feel it. And it makes them cry. And Jesus weeps with them.

What does Jesus show the people in the story about death? Not that it doesn't happen, not that it doesn't smell bad, not that it's not really sad. There's death. Real death. And despair. Real despair. And vulnerability, and creatureliness, brokeness, frailty, and everything we want to reject. Lazarus is dead. A dead person can't do *anything* for himself. He can't save himself. There's no good work that Lazarus can perform anymore. There is no possibility left for Lazarus. He is not, no way, at all, big and strong. He is as broken as broken can be, as weak and powerless as anyone could ever be. *He is dead.* But Jesus calls him, "Lazarus, come out of the tomb." And the man that was totally dead, totally helpless, stands up and comes out. And Jesus says "unbind him and let him go."

I think Jesus wants to show the people, us, everyone, that nothing can separate us from the love of God. Not death. Nothing we do or don't do, nothing past, nothing present, nothing to come, not powers, not weakness, not anything anywhere at all ever. God doesn't reject us in our utter brokenness no matter how dead. Rather, God gives us life again and again and love again and again. And death is no match for the love of God.

Resurrection. It's not that easy to believe maybe. It's a crazy story, but it seems to be the Christian story. God doesn't reject what we seem to consider to be the shameful secret at the core of our creatureliness: that we will become weak and die. Jesus doesn't deny death, but looks it full in the face and shows it to be what it is. Not God, not the final horrible, biggest truth, but rather an opportunity for resurrection. From death: life. Out of hopelessness, hope. If we could trust this, put our hope in resurrection, serve resurrection instead of death, if we trusted that God was God not death, maybe we could live more fully as who we are.

In the gospel of John, Jesus comes, it says, so that we might have life and have it abundantly. Maybe we could live more alive, more awake, embracing and loving and accepting fragile, creaturely, humanity. Maybe we could live much more humanely. Without our denial and repression maybe it would be difficult to live real comfortably within polite societal norms, difficult to be particularly at ease with the routines that the social order prescribes. But maybe that's the point, the hope, the goal.

If we were unprotected by what usually shields us from our inevitable and basic creaturely vulnerability, we might find that thoughtless, automatic living in the world was impossible. And it seems like that would be a really good thing. To resist culture's perpetual will to power, to resist the inevitable societal favor for the strong over the weak, the rich over the poor, the powerful over the powerless. Living fully and really awake might involve more fear and trembling and crying and fragility than we're comfortable with. I don't know. But I think when we are told on Ash Wednesday, "Remember, you are dust and you will return to dust," it's not to terrify us, but to free us to live and to hope in and to serve resurrection.

Leave Her Alone

April 2, 2001: Fifth Sunday of Lent

～

Six days before the Passover Jesus came to Bethany, the home of Lazarus, whom he had raised from the dead. There they gave a dinner for him. Martha served, and Lazarus was one of those at the table with him. Mary took a pound of costly perfume made of pure nard, anointed Jesus's feet, and wiped them with her hair. The house was filled with the fragrance of the perfume. But Judas Iscariot, one of his disciples (the one who was about to betray him), said, "Why was this perfume not sold for three hundred denarii and the money given to the poor?" (He said this not because he cared about the poor, but because he was a thief; he kept the common purse and used to steal what was put into it.) Jesus said, "Leave her alone. She bought it so that she might keep it for the day of my burial. You always have the poor with you, but you do not always have me."—John 12:1-8

I don't know if there's much sexual innuendo that makes us that uncomfortable anymore in this culture, although, in church maybe it wouldn't take much, certainly if we're talking about Jesus it wouldn't take that much. Whatever it would take for us, I think it would have taken a lot less for people in the first century and for a short little story this one seems to be packed full of it. With Mary and her long hair and Jesus's feet and the scented oil. I mean imagine this story in a culture where women aren't really supposed to eat in the same room with men and men aren't supposed to touch wet objects that women have touched much less actually touch women (other than of course their wives but even then there were restrictions) and where women were expected to wear their hair braided always in public unless they meant to advertise that they were a prostitute. This seems like a flagrantly uncomfortable story.

Right before this, Jesus has raised Lazarus, a friend whom he loved, from the dead. This story takes place at a dinner, maybe in honor of Lazarus, at least the text makes a point of mentioning his resurrection and his presence. Lazarus's sisters, Mary and Martha, are there. Martha is dutifully behaving exactly as women were expected to. Mary on the other hand, is pretty much doing nothing that would be the least bit expected. She's washing Jesus's feet.

Maybe you think, "oh they did that all the time," and people did wash their feet all the time, but generally you washed your own feet. Besides being very personal, feet are also very sensitive. Imagine someone washing your feet—it's intimate and sensual. Slaves sometimes washed their masters feet, but other than that people simply did not wash each others feet (at least in public). You could, and people do, read Mary's forward and unusual gesture as all about being "a slave." She's showing her humble subservience, she's acting like his slave by washing Jesus's feet.

Well...yeah, but with the perfume and the hair down and the hair drying the feet, she's almost certainly also acting a little affectionate, a little like a lover (c'mon).

The perfume (the fragrant ointment of pure nard) is not something that was a regular feature of foot washing, and adding it to the foot washing thing makes the whole thing even hotter. There are Greek plays of the era that ridicule the debauchery of exactly this sort of thing: Comic, self indulgent characters who revel in having young slave women caress their feet with perfume, say things like, "ah, to have my feet rubbed and perfumed with fair soft hands, isn't it magnificent?"

If this sort of thing was outlandish debauchery for the Greeks (who were generally fairly debauched) imagine what this scene must have seemed like to the Hebrews (who were generally puritanical in comparison).

Not only did Mary let down her hair, not only did she wash Jesus's feet, not only was there perfume involved but she actually perfumes her hair from the scented oil she has rubbed on Jesus's feet. That's not very puritanical sounding. So much about this story is so completely out of bounds that it seems surreal. This woman where women aren't supposed to be, doing what she's not supposed to be doing, water and feet and hair and the smell of perfume permeating everything.

Imagine a *pound* of perfume. It's hard to imagine because all you ever see is an ounce or two or maybe five, but never a pound. I can hardly stand to be in an elevator with someone who has one dab of perfume on their wrist. It seems like it would be nauseating to be in a house where someone was pouring a pound of it on someone's feet.

It's really an impossibly enormous amount of perfume. It's not even luxurious, it's comic. It's so exaggerated, it's nearly obscene.

Apparently it was worth what would be a decent year's wages. Imagine thirty thousand dollars of perfume poured out at once in an enclosed space (actually while people were trying to eat dinner). This is beyond lavish. This is unreasonable. This is not a rational act.

Everything about this is so far from prudent or careful or well conceived or chaste or modest. It doesn't make sense.

What does make sense, is that the whole thing would arouse indignation. It's so excessive, it's nearly lewd. Judas's response is perfectly understandable. I'm sure everyone was thinking along the same lines, "Mary, jeez, get a hold of yourself, contain yourself, have a little dignity, show some restraint, make sense, jeez."

Judas says "Why was this ointment not sold for three hundred denari and given to the poor?" This line of questioning under the circumstances seems pretty restrained to me. I mean you practically expect some incensed red-faced mad puritan to have her burnt at the stake, to stand up and barrage her with degrading expletives. Judas's question sounds merely responsible and prudent and rational and reasonable. Like, "Mary, what is the point? Make it have a point."

The question seems so...*right*. It's like, oh, you want to give something to God? Well make it practical, make it count for something. Make a decent pious sensible gesture, not some overly sentimental, emotional, superfluous, inappropriate, excessive, embarrassing-for-everybody gesture.

It's interesting, however, that this argument against Mary's act, an argument, that seems like an honest pious conviction, an argument which seems eminently sensible and reasonable and good...it's interesting that it's put into the mouth of Judas, the betrayer, and made into a lie.

What you would think was right (one ought to feed the poor) turns out, in this case, to be a lie and a betrayal. The author breaks in to tell us that actually Judas didn't really care for the poor.

I have to admit it's a little weird to think of Jesus in all this. Was he comfortable? Or uncomfortable? Did he enjoy it? Did he look away? You can't really ignore someone washing your feet with their hair. But all that is clear, all that we learn from the text, is that Jesus took Mary's side. He didn't go with the standard ethical thing, or the appropriate cultural thing, or what would seem to everybody to be *right*. He goes with her. Stands by her. Takes her side. He says, "Leave her alone. Let her be. Let her keep it for my burial. The poor you always have with you, but you do not always have me."

However uncomfortably outside the bounds this all was, how inappropriately sensual, Jesus clearly reads Mary's act as love, and far from rejecting it (because it was somehow unseemly, unorthodox, irrational) he gives it value she couldn't even know it had. She's not wasting perfume, not wasting anything. She's anointing him for his salvific act, preparing his body for burial. What seemed like a sexualized encounter because of its "inappropriate" intimacy becomes, in the context of the gospel of John, the exemplary act of love, an essential glimpse into what it means to be a disciple of Christ.

You could (and the church often does) look entirely at the "slave" aspect: she was willing to act as Jesus'ss slave. Mary was so piously humble and subservient that she was willing to bow down before Jesus, demean herself, sacrifice her most valued possession. You want to know how to be a disciple? Look at Mary, how pious and devout and virtuous and sacrificial she was. Be that, do that, calculate that.

But somehow, it seems like that's not quite it. It's not calculated virtue. It seems like she responds to Jesus with uncalculating, unselfconscious, extravagant attention: with love. Maybe she didn't have to construct a posture. Maybe she loved him. Maybe this was an authentic act of love. Maybe discipleship is like that.

Clearly in the Gospel of John discipleship is defined by acts of love. This is one. So from this look at it, what does "love" look like? Not some idea, some virtuous platonic ideal, some arid devotion. Not something exactly all rational and sensible and ethically derived. It doesn't seem like it's devoid of emotion and passion and sensuality.

The prophets in the Hebrew Scripture were constantly reminding the people that God desires love not sacrifice, relationship not burnt offerings, intimate knowledge. In Hosea, God is depicted as an abandoned, suffering husband yearning for his unfaithful wife, his beloved. I think Mary's act takes us to similar territory. God actually loves. And wants love, really. That's what it's about.

In the passage immediately preceding this one Jesus raised Mary's brother Lazarus from the dead. It's not explicit in the text, but it seems implicit to me, that part of what she does and feels is a response to that. If Jesus had just raised someone I loved from the dead (brought someone back to me that I loved), I would wash his feet (with my hair if it were long enough). I would bathe him in a pound of costly ointment.

If what we hear from this text (if what we learn or believe or feel) is that what God wants of us is for us to get down on our knees in a demeaning posture and perform a demeaning act, if we believe this is what it means to worship God, to be a disciple of Jesus, it might make us feel all sorts of things: a little afraid, maybe angry or disgusted or apathetic or entirely offended but I doubt it would make us love.

But what if that's not what it means to be a disciple. What if being a disciple is an authentic response to being loved. And what if being loved...actually feels like being loved. Not like some abstract belief we adhere to, not like something so-called-purely-spiritual, as if there could be such a thing, but something that has to do with the part of us that thirsts and hungers and feels and suffers and loves and cries, our passions, our needs, what is thoroughly and essentially human in us.

Maybe God didn't bring your brother back to life, raise him from the dead, but maybe we can glimpse somehow from this story that God's love is *that good*. God's love is that connected to what we need, to our guts, to our passion, to our essential primal humanness. And worshipping, loving God—is our natural real uncalculated, unselfconscious response to that love. Maybe God's love is that good, not something you have to talk yourself into believing in. And the disciples response is not something you have to fake. To love Jesus doesn't mean to respond to a demand to be subservient, to fall on your knees in devout piety, it's a response to a love that is *that* good that you want to, that you will.

Just a little bit later on in the story, Jesus does for his disciples almost precisely what Mary did for him. During a meal with his disciples he takes off all his clothes, wraps a towel around his loins, pours water into a basin, and begins to wash the disciples' feet, wiping their feet with the towel which he was using to cover himself.

That's a crazy story to tell to illustrate the love of God. That love doesn't seem to be devoid of emotion and passion and sensuality. How excessive for God to go this far. It's immodest, nearly lewd. It makes sense that the whole thing would arouse indignation. How could God be so immodest and insensible, to not only become incarnate in the world, to chase after us in this way, but to expose his loins as he washes the disciples feet. To suffer and die naked on a cross. You would think that God would show a little more restraint than that, retain more dignity, do something more decent and pious and sensible than such a seemingly uncontained expression of passionate love.

I don't know exactly how you come to feel that towel on your feet. Maybe eating bread and drinking wine, maybe the way the sky looks at five in the morning, maybe cerulean, cornflower, azure, turquoise, ultramarine, maybe not, maybe not at all. But even if you don't know it or feel it or seem to have access to it, maybe it's still true that God loves us passionately. And because of that, we will love the Lord God with all our hearts and souls and minds. It's not about constructing a posture. It's about being who you are, the beloved.

Res[E]rection

November 11, 2001: Twentey-fifth Sunday of Pentecost

~

Some Sadducees, those who say there is no resurrection, came to him and asked him a question, "Teacher, Moses wrote for us that if a man's brother dies, leaving a wife but no children, the man shall marry the widow and raise up children for his brother. Now there were seven brothers; the first married and died childless; then the second and the third married her, and so in the same way all seven died childless. Finally the woman also died. In the resurrection whose wife will she be? For the seven had married her." Jesus said to them, "Those who belong to this age marry and are given in marriage; but those who are considered worthy of a place in that age and in the resurrection from the dead neither marry nor are given in marriage. Indeed they cannot die anymore, because they are like angels and are children of God, being children of the resurrection. And the fact that the dead are raised Moses himself showed, in the story about the bush, where he speaks of the Lord as the God of Abraham, the God of Isaac, and the God of Jacob. Now he is God not of the dead, but of the living; for to him all of them are alive." Then some of the scribes answered, "Teacher you have spoken well." For they no longer dared to ask him another question.—Luke 20:27-40

Driving home last week, I got a little worked up over an underwriter's slogan I heard on NPR. It was something like, *Underwritten by ADM Soy Products, The Nature of What's to Come.* I thought, "So. That's the nature of what's to come. World peace? The end of poverty? No. Soy products. Great." I thought, how hopelessly banal. How pathetic. Humanity is doomed.

I think it was just the last straw in this string of reports on the attempt to develop a better anthrax vaccine, new security measures at airports, equipment to irradiate mail. It seemed like these were all such paltry little attempts to save people, make a good future, make hope. It seemed like this was not news. It was so not news, it was olds. It was redundant and tedious and not at all hopeful. And now does Archer Daniel Midlands mean to suggest somehow that *soy products* might comprise the scope of our dreams, hopes, and solutions?

If we're going to envision *The Nature of What's to Come,* as all about new technology, airport security measures, bio-engineered soy, then our dreams are so dull, our solutions hopelessly redundant, our hopes delusive, and there is nothing new, no news, really. So I turned off *All Things Considered* and considered and considered a zillion times over, and put on some gospel music to expand the hope to a little broader plane and pledged to never put my hope in soy anything.

Of course, there are plenty of people who think the hope you might find in the gospel story is pretty dull and delusive and fraudulent, even. The text we read tonight comes at the end of a whole series of challenges to Jesus. It's like all sorts of people who thought it was crazy or stupid or delusive to believe in Jesus have lined up to try and expose him as a false authority, as nobody particularly special, as politically incorrect.

The challenge in our story comes from a group of guys, the Sadducees, who are bothered that anyone would believe in anything as ludicrous as resurrection. Their intent seems to be to expose Jesus as maybe a little stupid, as a fool. He believes in resurrection.

Nobody knows very much about the Sadducees, but they seem to have been fairly influential, successful, probably pretty wealthy, somewhat religious though not pious or rigid like the Pharisees. Maybe more culturally accommodating, smart, successful, savvy sort of guys who enjoyed witty banter, clever arguments, maybe an occasional cigar, leather furniture, men's clubs and scotch and some good-natured laughs over the quaint beliefs of the not-so-smart and irrational traditions of the not-so-successful.

I don't really know what they were like. But it's pretty clear that the story they concoct and pose to Jesus, in the form of a mocking question, is meant to make fun of belief in resurrection.

"Teacher," they say, "Moses gave us a sensible practical little law meant to ensure that a man's seed lives on after he dies, even if he never had a son in his lifetime. The brother of the dead man is supposed to take the dead man's widow and give her his seed (you know) so that she might have a son who would then bear the dead man's name, so the dead man's name will live on in Israel.

"Well, Jesus, say the first brother died, and there was still no son, so the second brother takes the woman and gives her his seed, still no son. Then he died. The third brother takes her. Dies. No son. And the fourth, the same thing. And the fifth the same thing. And the sixth the same thing. And the seventh takes her and gives her his seed. Dies and there is still no success. Finally the woman dies barren.

"Well, it's a good thing isn't it Jesus that there's a *resurrection*" and they're winking and nudging each other, "because how else would that first poor man ever have any hope of living on? Thank goodness we have the resurrection for all the poor sterile buggers and barren wives who can't *produce* anything significant in this life, poor fellows, who never come to anything, who are unable to make any significant contribution to our society, just can't quite get it going on down here, can't get things growing, if you know what I mean. Well it's a good thing you have the res[e]rection for all those unfortunate flaccid losers now isn't it?"

"But one thing, one small problem, Jesus, Moses doesn't seem to have made any provisions for resurrection in the law. So then, in the resurrection, whose wife will the woman be? You know, the barren woman who has been with seven men. Who will she belong to?"

I don't know, but the Sadducees may have smirked or sniggered or giggled or something at this point. At any rate it's doubtful that they were able to act entirely serious: it's not so serious a question. But now they get quiet, because there's this big long pause, waiting for Jesus to respond.

And Jesus is just, like, I don't know, petting his camel (sort of methodically combing through clumps of dirt with his fingers) and after a long pause, he looks up, and he says, "Did you ask me whose *wife* will that woman be?" And he kind of lets out a long breath of air, "Pheww," and he does a sort of combination of an incredulous, impatient, and mocking look at them, "That woman? I think she may grow wings in the kingdom. A little like a Luna moth. But more colorful maybe. That woman? She may be queen bee in the kingdom. She may fly. Her name may be sung by jewel-like little birds everywhere. She may populate an entire country with daughters. But one thing's for sure, she won't *belong* to any man."

Jesus doesn't answer their question on their terms. He doesn't enter the scenario they create. He ushers in an entirely new landscape. And he sets the woman free.

He says, "Maybe you can't quite imagine it, but resurrection isn't just the same old same old, except bigger, or louder or see-through, or up in heaven or something. We're not talking about the realm of flat squares, of institutions, of security measures and vaccines. It's not what you already know, or something you can handle, like you handle facts and information."

Resurrection is a genuinely new thing. Beyond any scenario you can create. It's not like bell bottoms or mustaches, or volkswagon beetles, coming back again in new colors, or shapes. It's God doing an entirely new thing. Making hope out of a situation of no hope. Creating something from nothing. It's life out of death. You may say it's delusive, but you can't say it's dull.

Jesus goes on to show them that though they may have thought the resurrection was just some inessential, sort of stupid, unnecessary add-on to faith in God, it's actually always been essential to God's very nature. God is a God of resurrection.

Moses is recognizing this, according to Jesus, when he calls God the God of Abraham, Isaac, and Jacob. Because Abraham, Isaac, and Jacob's stories are all stories about God overcoming sterility and barrenness with fertility and life. Abraham married Sarah and she could have no children. Isaac married Rebecca and her womb was closed. Jacob married Rachel but she was barren. The stories of the patriarchs, of the Hebrew Bible, are always about human effort and endeavor proving futile, but about God giving life to the dead. God calling into existence what does not exist. It's always about sterility, barrenness, death being overcome by divine passion and love and mercy. The story of God? It's always about resurrection: God pursuing and caring for God's people past any limit life or death might pose.

And after that, apparently, all the people waiting to challenge Jesus decide they better go brush up on their Jewish history, or that he's not so dumb or they like him, or they're afraid of him. At any rate, the text says, no one dared ask him any more questions.

The Sadduccees meant to mock Jesus. But Jesus points to a possibility beyond necessity that actually sort of mocks their limited vision of life, of everything.

It may be that the Sadducees had a hard time not believing that death was the real limit, the ultimate limit, the greatest power in a way, the big thing that stops everything. C'mon, nothing could really defeat death. Death is undefeatable. Resurrection is absurd. It's pretty common, I think, to feel that way.

But actually, as threatening as death might seem, at least we know what it looks like. Resurrection is a little unnerving, unsettling, because it basically goes against what we know, contradicts everything we take to be absolute about the nature of history and the reality in which we live. It's a toppling of earthly order, overthrowing familiarity. It doesn't play according to the rules we accept as necessary. If the dead can come back to life, if that (sort of major) rule is broken, what does that mean about all the other realities, rules, that order our lives, that we take for granted?

Resurrection is a little threatening. I think maybe because the order of the universe as we know it probably includes a few things that we have sort of come to count on. Work hard? You'll make it in the world. Your status counts for something. Jesus shocked the Sadduccees by suggesting that resurrection topples the absolute patriarchal rule, where women belonged to men. That rule (along with a lot of others) was probably working just fine for them. And there are probably plenty of ways in which the order of the world may actually be working out pretty well for us.

I think it would be safe to say that all of us here enjoy privilege conferred on us by the way the world is ordered. Such apocalyptic ideas like resurrection are unsettling because they threaten the world as we know it, status quo, what we count on, how we're used to ordering, power and privilege. Resurrection isn't like some personal insurance policy that you can earn by believing in God, or something. It's not just reassurance for individuals hoping to slip by death's vast powers somehow. Resurrection sucks all the power from death. It is God overcoming every obstacle to love and mercy. Resurrection isn't an individual's ticket to the afterlife, resurrection turns the world upside down.

It may not be perfectly safe, but it opens us to the possibility of genuine surprise, to grace and love that confound the limits of all our calculations, the limits of all our "orders". The Sadducees may have been really smart, maybe supremely, even infallibly logical, but they lacked something, enough imagination, or something (probably faith), to believe in the un-limited, boundless, commitment God has to God's creation, the infinite reach of God's liberating love and grace. I kind of suspect I lack whatever that is too. But Jesus'ss whole thing is to try and get them (and us) to glimpse it, know it, see signs of it here and now. It isn't just about life after death. It's about nothing being able to separate us from the love of God, not life, or death, or power, or principalities, not now or ever.

It's not everything you already know. It's not what you hear from Dan Rather on the nightly news. It's a whole different landscape. It's not genetically modified soy products. It's not new security measures or vac-cines. It's not predictable. It's a word that uncloses, makes open, breaks certitude. It's possibility overwhelming necessity. It's actual bona fide good news.

Waiting for Something to Happen
November 10, 2002: Twenty-fifth Sunday of Pentecost

~

"Then the kingdom of heaven will be like this. Ten bridesmaids took their lamps and went to meet the bridegroom. Five of them were foolish, and five were wise. When the foolish took their lamps, they took no oil with them; but the wise took flasks of oil with their lamps. As the bridegroom was delayed, all of them became drowsy and slept. But at midnight there was a shout, 'Look! Here is the bridegroom! Come out to meet him.' Then all those bridesmaids got up and trimmed their lamps. The foolish said to the wise, 'Give us some of your oil, for our lamps are going out.' But the wise replied, 'No! there will not be enough for you and for us; you had better go to the dealers and buy some for yourselves.' And while they went to buy it, the bridegroom came, and those who were ready went with him into the wedding banquet; and the door was shut. Later the other bridesmaids came also, saying, 'Lord, Lord, open to us.' But he replied, 'Truly I tell you, I do not know you.' Keep awake therefore, for you know neither the day nor the hour."—Matthew 25:1-13

"Keep awake, for you know neither the day nor the hour." Maybe that's good news for the world, but you have to admit that it could be an ad for a scary movie. It depends on where your mind goes: Freddy Krueger or the kingdom of God. Or unfortunately, I guess there is the possibility of mixing the two up a little so you get a strange genre of Christian Horror. It seems to sell really well these days. I looked it up on Amazon.com: "Christian Horror." You can buy any number of novels, videos, and cassettes along with a vast array of related merchandise. I'm not kidding.

I'm not really into the Christian Horror genre myself, but still, these are not my favorite sorts of passages in the Bible. I like the "don't be anxious for tomorrow for tomorrow will take care of itself," sorts of passages. Something a little more obviously full of love and mercy, something incapable of spinning a horror book series, maybe something a little less urgent.

But these sorts of passages are urgent and they are meant to create some tension, like "wake up, come on." What's most tense, I think, is that the tension seems unending. Something is going to happen and you don't know when and the thing that's going to happen keeps not happening. At least in a movie the tension builds, the music gets all crazy, your heart races a little, and then the *thing* happens, and it's over and your body relaxes. But with this waiting for the coming of the Lord, the moment of waiting seems to never be over.

This parable about the maidens and the lamps seems to say, "So you have to keep waiting? Well then, you have to stay prepared. Stay prepared always. Be perpetually prepared." That does sound like horror. It sounds horrible to me. It sounds at least very, very stressful. I can hardly manage to keep enough gas in the car or milk in the refrigerator. I can't keep my son supplied with enough clean socks. I have not returned a video or a library book on time for years. I can't really imagine being perpetually prepared for anything. Be prepared always. That doesn't sound like good news. That sounds like something that might send a person off in search of heroin.

But then, maybe the call to keep awake, be prepared, get ready isn't really reducible to a call for me to get my life together. As if it was all about, "Okay, Debbie, you must get more organized. Now, look, just be sure to carry around a supply of extra oil. It's not that hard. Just get with it for God's sake."

There are some things that it's crazy for people to even try to talk about. Probably a lot of what we try to talk about in church is a little like that. But this "waiting for the day of the Lord" is some crazy stuff. Apocalyptic eschatology, God's coming at the close of the age. Jesus coming again in the clouds. The end of time. The kingdom of heaven. There aren't really any very good or adequate words to say what it is we wait for, much less good words to describe how to prepare for it. Be ready, prepare for...what? What does it mean to be prepared for something as mysterious, impossible to imagine, as hard to believe in, as "the culmination of time" or God coming? How do you "get ready" for something you can hardly even imagine or describe. What's it like?

Is it like the urgency you feel when you know the guests will be arriving any moment? Is it the sort of getting ready that almost always involves yelling at the children for tracking in mud for the fortieth time? Does it feel like having just fifteen minutes to finish the dishes, whip the cream, shower, put the music on, light the candles, and (most crucially) change your attitude? The guests may arrive momentarily and you must move from the mode of frenzied physical preparation to that of gracious reception. You have about two minutes to get happy. If you don't succeed? It's possible that you will wreck everything.

I have really found that the key to successful readiness in this sort of situation is to open the wine early. Start your glass maybe half an hour before the guests arrive. But, just think. What if you have no control over, no idea when the guests will arrive. You don't know the hour, the day, the year. You just have to be perpetually prepared, constantly keeping the floor mud free, the house in good shape. The kids track in mud. You clean it up. They track it in. You clean it up, on and on and you must be gracious and kind. If this is the Christian life, it seems like a recipe for insanity or unbelievable stress or complete alcoholism.

Matthew tells a story to try and get at what it might be like to wait, to prepare, to be ready. I don't know that I completely get his story, but it's nothing like that stress scenario. It's not like having everything in order, bills paid, dishes done, will written, hands/body/soul clean. It's like ten maidens, he says, who took their lamps and went to meet the bridegroom. Not ten frenzied fundies, worried for their souls. Not ten harried hostesses snapping at their children. Not eight maids a milking, seven swans a swimming, but ten young "virgins" actually (the text says) waiting eagerly for a man to arrive. Doesn't that have a little different feel to it? I mean, I don't know if Matthew meant *that*, but these young women are not apparantly overburdened with responsibilities. They are not worrying about mud in the entry way, whipping the cream or preparing the feast. They don't have children. Not only do they not have children, they're a little bit like childen. They aren't the adults in charge anyway. It's the day of a huge celebration: music, food, dancing and fancy dresses. Moms taking good smelling things out of the oven, and it all culminates with the arrival of the bridegroom.

Waiting for God? It's like the young girls going out to meet the bridegroom with their lamps. The youngsters often get the best of that kind of thing. They get so excited, not like stressed ever, just beautifully and childishly excited. The image is less like grown ups with brooms, than it is kids out at night, looking around with their flashlights, anticipating some unknown, new and amazing, event. And childlike anticipation is so different than adult-like anticipation. It's untainted by much memory of disappointment.

But the bridegroom doesn't come and doesn't come and doesn't come and eventually, as much as it seemed that the pure wonder of it all would keep them awake infinitely? It doesn't. They get weary. The bridegroom doesn't come and doesn't come and doesn't come. Excitement wanes. The bridegroom doesn't come and doesn't come and doesn't come and eventually the maids get a little older, a little fatter, a little less childlike. They get just a few crow's-fcct by their eyes waiting for the culmination of all things, the kingdom of heaven, the coming of the Lord.

The bridegroom doesn't come and doesn't come but eventually, they've seen a lot of other grooms come and go. Eventually they've been to a lot of weddings. And it's not that weddings are bad or they don't like them, but they do quit anticipating that it's some miraculous fulfillment, the zenith of all possibility.

The bridegroom doesn't come and doesn't come and doesn't come. Eventually they get married themselves, nurse several children, their dresses don't fit anymore, and they quit anticipating that the whole event really has that much to offer. I think that's just a little what it's like living in time, growing up.

I don't know about you, but I sort of feel like I want to say to the these girls, "You know what? Go home, little sisters. I'm sorry but I don't think it's going to be worth your wait. You may get in on a little bit of a feast, but what are you waiting for? It's not even your man, and even if it was... I mean, you just start to know things, and it just starts to seem like there's a lot better things you might do with your time than keeping a lamp lit, waiting for some groom to come, so you can light his way to a wedding feast." I mean, come on.

If the foolish ones run out of oil, it's the most unsurprising thing in the world if you ask me. I mean who really has the kind of fuel to keep that crazy excitement going forever? And I don't know if they even seem that foolish. It sort of seems like anyone very smart would have dumped the lamps and gone to bed hours ago, years ago, centuries ago.

If the "wise ones" have some kind of fuel that keeps their lamps perpetually lit? Well, I just wonder what that oil is, and where in the world do you get it? It must be some oil. I guess Matthew calls them "wise" but it doesn't seem like a word that is entirely adequate, exactly perfectly right. I mean, I'm not trying to be hard on them but they do display some slightly stupid and selfish traits.

They won't share their oil with their friends for one. And they tell them to go out and buy some from the stores even though it's midnight. I mean c'mon, where do you buy that oil? Buy it? C'mon. The shops are closed, shut down. But I don't think it's the kind of thing you're going to find in the mall anyway. Even at noon, they aren't selling it at Target. You can't order it from Amazon.com. I'm sure of that. Where do you get that kind of oil?

But the foolish ones do actually go and try to buy it. Which I guess is equally if not much more foolish than just saying you should try to buy it. And they miss the arrival of the groom. And when they try to get into the wedding feast, when they say, "Open the door!" The groom says, "I don't know you," which is probably true. I mean he didn't go to school with them. They weren't there when he arrived. He may not even be from the neighborhood. It's not necessarily a doctrinal statement about God shutting the door forever on the people who don't believe quite how you believe, it's not a treatise on hell, but it's the end of this parable.

Be prepared. Be ready. Keep awake. Awake to what? The need to keep the mud out, keep your home in order? Prepared, how? By seeing to it that you've accomplished all that needs to be accomplished. Could it be that all along the prophets, Jesus, have been calling the people to live by the grace of God, but now when Matthew says "be ready" he means, "batten the hatches or you're going down." "You! get that oil now, or it's all over." I don't think so.

It seems like the oil is the key to readiness. It's the oil that keeps the lamp burning. The ones who've got it are the ones who are prepared. So. Where do you get that oil? It's pretty clear from what comes before and after this story in Matthew, that wherever you get the oil, the light burning is living a life full of deeds of love and mercy: giving the hungry food, the thirsty, something to drink, welcoming strangers. But later in this chapter you see that the ones who lived this life, according to Jesus, don't even recognize themselves as the ones who are ready.

Mattthew says, "Let your light shine before people that they may see your good works and give glory to God." What kind of shining is that? It's unusual. What kind of readiness is it where you might not even be aware of being ready? Seems like something the last and the least may do more readily than the first and the best.

What fuels the undying lamp? Your good deeds? Your ability to prepare, your ability to secure the disposition of your eternal soul? Perpetual fear? Perpetual anxiety? I don't think so. I think the oil isn't that different from what the whole scripture pretty much always says is indispensable to life: the grace of God. And to have an extra store of oil, to have wisdom, is trust in God. That wisdom may appear a little foolish. A lot of things seem smarter and maybe more logically sound. It might seem foolish to trust that despite everything time has taught you, despite your cynicism, and disappointment, it might seem foolish to trust inspite of all that, that mercy and love and grace will be the final victor. But I think that's what Matthew is calling us to do here.

Not to make our deeds shine before the world, but to trust that love and mercy and the grace of God will be the final word. And maybe somehow, if you're doing that, if you trust that, your light shines not like the Pharisees who must have their good deeds known to everybody, but like the lamps of the maidens, illuminating not your way, but the way of the bridegroom: the love and mercy and grace of God.

Do you have oil? Were you created out of the love of God for love? Do you live in the mercy, by the grace of God? You do. Keep awake.

Zeta Fino Flora Fennel

November 14, 1999: Twenty-fifth Sunday of Pentecost

~

"For it is as if a man, going on a journey, summoned his slaves and entrusted his property to them; to one he gave five talents, to another two, to another one, to each according to his ability. Then he went away. The one who had received the five talents went off at once and traded with them, and made five more talents. In the same way, the one who had the two talents made two more talents. But the one who had received the one talent went off and dug a hole in the ground and hid his master's money. After a long time the master of those slaves came and settled accounts with them. Then the one who had received the five talents came forward, bringing five more talents, saying, 'Master, you handed over to me five talents; see, I have made five more talents.' His master said to him, 'Well done, good and trustworthy slave; you have been trustworthy in a few things, I will put you in charge of many things; enter into the joy of your master.' And the one with the two talents also came forward, saying, 'Master, you handed over to me two talents; see, I have made two more talents.' His master said to him, 'Well done, good and trustworthy slave; you have been trustworthy in a few things, I will put you in charge of many things; enter into the joy of your master.' Then the one who had received the one talent also came forward, saying, 'Master, I knew that you were a harsh man, reaping where you did not sow, and gathering where you did not scatter seed; so I was afraid, and I went and hid your talent in the ground. Here you have what is yours.' But his master replied, 'You wicked and lazy slave! You knew, did you, that I reap where I did not sow, and gather where I did not scatter? Then you ought to have invested my money with the bankers, and on my return I would have received what was my own with interest. So take the talent from him, and give it to the one with the ten talents. For to all those who have, more will be given, and they will have an abundance; but from those who have nothing, even what they have will be taken away. As for this worthless slave, throw him into the outer darkness, where there will be weeping and gnashing of teeth.'"—Matthew 25: 14-30*

Okay, so you can flip a switch and virtually be anywhere in the world immediately. And you can get all the nutrients you need in a single bite of some mega bar thing. And you can even get your caffeine in water. But if you want a latte? You can get one at the 7-11 while you fill your tank. You want revolution? There's actually a shop. It's on your right as you're going down Lyndale.

But let's just say everything worth having isn't immediately accessible, that there is something we might want to watch for, something not already completely in our own hands, something that eludes our grasp.

Say we wait. What is it like living like that? I mean if it's really true that what we know isn't everything, then, what's it like "in the meantime"? We should know what it's like, I guess, because that's where we live. But maybe it will reveal something about our situation to imagine for a moment it's like, Great Grandma Eisley was going on a journey.

Grandma Eisley was the matriarch of this little farming community. She had an incredible garden, stuff you wouldn't believe, stuff you've never seen. She saved seeds. Seeds from her grandma and her grandma's grandma and some people said, and it was probably true, that she had seeds from tomatoes that grew in the Garden of Eden. I'm not kidding. She had seeds from plant varieties that had virtually vanished from the rest of the world.

Most people in town just grew their gardens from the hybrid variety seeds from big seed companies. Her seeds had never cross pollinated with anything even remotely genetically engineered. Every beet seed, pea, corn kernel, could be traced back to a long line of plants that had never even come in contact with any soil that had a trace of chemical fertilizer or pesticide. They were pure organic heirlooms. They were precious. Grandma Eisley's garden was a very rare treasure.

One spring Grandma Eisley decided to take a trip to Europe. Before she left she distributed her seed collection to various families in town and asked them to care for them. She didn't divide it up evenly because tit-for-tat-even-steven was never her big thing. It just looked to her like some people had more space than others.

It was the Freely family that got the most seeds. And well, looking at it from one angle you could say they were a little irresponsible. Careless. It was almost like it wasn't that big of a deal to them, like they didn't recognize the value of what they had. They just went out right away, even though it was a windy day, and spread the seed. It was reckless. As if they didn't even realize what might be lost if the wind blew and the century old Zeta Fino Flora Fennel cross pollinated with the neighbor's mutated soy beans.

And as the years passed (Grandma was gone a lot longer than anyone expected), the Freelys' garden grew sort of like crazy and wild and quite honestly, they weren't even that careful about weeding it. They had some funky looking squash that had to have been the result of, well, let's say, the purity had been clearly compromised. And besides that, they were kind of tacky.

They lined some of the flower beds with used tires. Imagine what that was leaching into the soil. And it didn't look that good. It didn't seem to be in the spirit of Grandma Eisley. The whole thing seemed like a mess, a big chaotic ugly mess. And when the fall came and they harvested seeds? Sure, they had a ton, but of what compromised variety?

It was actually pretty much the same story at the Wilders' place. Grandma had given them five bags of seeds. Both those families, frankly, just didn't seem that...smart. They didn't seem to be aware of the intricacies of the treasure they were supposed to be caring for.

But then there were the Shackleys. They got one bag of Grandma's seed and they knew how precious it was. They waited for a perfectly still morning. They buried each seed in a carefully prepared plot. Even if it was one of those itty bitty minute herb seeds? They covered it with just a fine layer of wet sand. They didn't lose even one grain of Spotted Medicinal Mint, or one dot of Creeping Green Mountain Oregano. They got a nice tasteful fence up right away. And they even populated it with a special variety of spiders whose webs helped catch invading pollen particles. They weeded it every day. Everything was all neat and gorgeous.

They kept the #552 French Horticultural Heirloom Pole Beans on the opposite side from the Mideast Prolific Cucumbers because they knew the cucumbers had a tendency to mingle with the beans. And it was really gorgeous.

They were immaculately responsible about preserving every seed variety from every possible corruption. The garden remained sort of small because, well, they just didn't let it go. But they always harvested just the right number of perfectly preserved seeds of absolutely uncompromised variety.

The years passed. (Like I said, Grandma didn't come back for a long time.) And as they waited, the Shackleys' garden became more of a preserve really. They had locks put on the gates. Not to keep people out, it was just that they began to worry that the neighbors might wander in carelessly with like, some seed company corn pollen stuck to their shoe. Eventually they even posted people at the gates to monitor the boot baths. See, they had these little things with sprays and brushes, sort of like a car wash for your feet. Really they were just acting in what they believed was the most responsible manner.

Every once in awhile they'd look out across the neighbor's fields and they'd think that the wild black-eyed Susans were beautiful and it wouldn't hurt a thing to let them in. But if they even *thought* that, they immediately reigned themselves in. They'd tell themselves, "Wait. Then why have we been working so hard to keep the dirt off our shoes?" Questioning the project was like the most insecure thing, so they'd just remind themselves that the soil out there was uncontrollable, really, and there was no telling what chemical residue any outside plant might carry. They were pretty successful at keeping any ambiguity from clouding their project.

After awhile it started to seem like Grandma was gone forever. It seemed less like they were really *waiting* for anything, and it began to be clear that the thing to do "in the meantime" was trust in what they knew and what they knew best was preserving seeds. Grandma had become a little ambiguous or something, just a lot less clear than the garden preservation project. And actually, after awhile, all their carefulness and vigilance began to generate a sort of fear. There began to be this sense that if they had to be so gol darn careful, and precise, and painstaking, and avoid making any mistakes, Grandma Eisley must be a hard and demanding old woman.

Actually, without their knowing even what was really happening, a specter began to hang over their pretty little garden. A specter of a cruel and merciless master, although they would never have articulated it that way. The reality was that they began to operate out of fear. And it got so everything they did, every move they made, was under this haunting specter of exacting judgment. They began to have the sense that they, their world, everything, was unsafe. The seed companies were just cranking out mutant varietals. There were rumors about monarchs carrying genetically altered chromosomes. But what made them confident and reassured, what made them feel safe,while they waited, was tending to the purity of the seeds.

So they waited and they did what they believed was demanded of them, trying harder and harder to assure themselves that "The Grandma" would be unable to charge them with losing even one heirloom seed. They were increasingly cautious people.

Now, after a long, long, long time, Grandma Eisley returned. When she walked onto the Freelys' farm, they were all sitting around eating God-knows-what pesticide ridden variety of peaches. They looked up, with peach juice dripping from their mouths, and they jumped up and said, "Oh my gosh. You're back. No way. Wow. Gosh. Wow. Come and see the garden?"

And they led her out to the fields and there it was. It was no longer five acres of certified organic heirloom plant varieties. By this time the Canadian Purple Pumpkin had spread over an entire acre of pesticide soil, the Pioneer Shell Peas (peas that had been preserved for several centuries) were vining up all over some neighbor's chemical corn crop. It was huge and unwieldy. There were weeds like crazy and Grandma looked out across the mess and she raised her fist and she said,

"My...goodness. That's," and she paused, "...beautiful.

"I like the canopy effect the pea vines have over the corn field.

"You know, you might want to be a little more careful where you plant the Walla Walla onions. I love what you did with those tires. That's nice. Creative. Kind of funky" (she learned to say "funky" in Europe).

She went over to where the weeds were ravaging the sweet cherry peppers and she got down on her knees and she said, "Let me help you pull a few weeds." And after they were all digging in the dirt awhile, she pulled them over to show them something they'd never seen before, this place where there were violets growing out of a bunch of dead rotted cucumbers. She showed them some gorgeous new strain of cantaloupe, that had sprung up out of the compost pile. And they'd never even seen it. And there was a lot of joy going around. And it was pretty much the same over at the Wilders' place.

After a beautiful morning and afternoon, Grandma made her way over to the Shackleys'. She had a little trouble getting in because the gate was locked, of course. But she finally found someone to let her in.

The Shackleys hardly recognized her. She looked so...unkempt...for such a persnickety lady, and sort of dirty, and she didn't even use the boot bath. But the Shackleys stepped forward and bowed low, real respectful, even trembling a little, because they were scared of her. But they felt pretty confident as they said, (and it seemed like maybe they'd rehearsed this quite a few times), "We knew how demanding and exacting you were. We knew what vigilance and care you required, so...here it is! It's all perfectly preserved. Not one drop of chemical fertilizer has spilled on this soil. And not one pollen from chemical corn anywhere has compromised the purity." Several Shackleys looked at Grandma's boots and *felt* like saying, "yeah, not until now." But they said, "Here, we knew you were hard and mean and greedy and exacting, have what is yours."

And Grandma felt...not good. And things got a little tense. It seems like sort of a crazy thing, but Grandma called all the Shackleys "wicked and slothful." Which seemed not really very accurate, but they did call her "hard and cruel and mean and exacting," which wasn't very accurate either. Her feelings were hurt, and maybe she wanted to reflect a little how it felt to her. She said, "You *knew* that I was exacting and hard hearted? Maybe you should have made sure you let the pepper varieties pollinate openly. Their nutritional content could have evolved. But, now, it's all just exactly the same."

And she shook her head and she cried as she looked at the scared, tight, defensive Shackleys. She said, "Look, it wasn't supposed to be about this. This isn't what I wanted—fences and locks and guards and sanitizing baths and...invulnerable...people. Pesticides break down eventually. The Zeta Fino Flora Fennel is a hearty species." She said, "Tear down the gates. Let the Wilders' broccoli and the Freelys' corn grow into the garden." And it seemed to the Shackleys like everything they had was taken away. They were dumbfounded. Their fences and gates and locks and sanitizing baths and their whole system of preservation was taken away. They felt lost, and in the dark, and they wept (and maybe they even gnashed their teeth a little.)

I don't think we're that great at waiting. We do all sorts of crazy things "in the meantime." And maybe when our movements are all about protecting and burying and fear and hiding and creating some invulnerable thing, they are not really about faith. Maybe these movements somehow contribute to a picture of a merciless world. But maybe if we keep trying to glimpse that merciful master? Maybe we'll grow some nice fruit, some cantaloupe, maybe out of the compost pile, without even trying.

Glory Doesn't Shine, It Bleeds

May 12, 2002: Seventh Sunday of Easter

❧

After Jesus had spoken these words, he looked up to heaven and said, "Father, the hour has come; glorify your Son so that the Son may glorify you, since you have given him authority over all people, to give eternal life to all whom you have given him. And this is eternal life, that they may know you, the only true God, and Jesus Christ whom you have sent. I glorified you on earth by finishing the work that you gave me to do. So now, Father, glorify me in your own presence with the glory that I had in your presence before the world existed. I have made your name known to those whom you gave me from the world. They were yours, and you gave them to me, and they have kept your word. Now they know that everything you have given me is from you; for the words that you gave to me I have given to them, and they have received them and know in truth that I came from you; and they have believed that you sent me. I am asking on their behalf; I am not asking on behalf of the world, but on behalf of those whom you gave me, because they are yours. All mine are yours, and yours are mine; and I have been glorified in them. And now I am no longer in the world, but they are in the world, and I am coming to you. Holy Father, protect them in your name that you have given me, so that they may be one, as we are one."—John 17: 1-11

I didn't really like that text from John when I first read it. I'm not crazy about the word "glory." I certainly wouldn't choose to use three versions of it six times in seven sentences...in a climactic moment of any story I was writing: glory, glorify, glorified, glorify thy, glorify thou, glorify thee. I don't even understand what it is.

Majesty. Splendor. Glory. They seem like names for dishwashing liquids. They seem like words you find in travel brochures that you pick up in rest areas. Ones that have been there for thirty years, with overexposed pictures of families by swimming pools. Brochures with statements like: "Enjoy the majesty of the Rocky Mountains while basking in the glory of our heated indoor pool."

Maybe it's just an old word, glory, and it used to be a great word. But it feels like an empty word to me. Hollow. And, I don't know, but I think it's a word that calls up some inkling of suspicion in me, too. Glory. What kind of God cares so much about his own glory, or her own glory? Zeus maybe, or Aphrodite, some God with long blond hair or some God with muscles. Some God who demands constant homage.

It seems like the kind of God who would care so much about his glory is the kind of God who would get really pissed at a trifle, a slight. Like he might overhear someone say he's really not that good looking and make it rain for forty days. Or keeps the wind blowing in a certain direction for forty years and sailors have to make sacrifices to appease him, placate him, smooth his ruffled feathers. It seems like that's the kind of God who cares about glory.

Or maybe like Snow White's evil stepmother, or aunt, or whoever: the queen in Snow White, who goes to the mirror every day to make sure it's still certain that she's the fairest of them all. I mean, I know the feeling, but could you trust a God like that? A God who was motivated by that? Look what happens to Snow White when she threatens the queen's glory (just by being her beautiful self). The queen is determined that she must die. Could a God like that possibly help us, care for us, love us? A God obsessed with being worshiped, obsessed with glory, his beauty, his muscles, his hair?

Okay. So. The text for today has glory all over it. Practically every other word. Jesus praying to be glorified. Glorify thee. Glorify me. It's a prayer for glory. I felt like it was a little hard to get into that. Makes me want to shut the book. Throw it out the window. I don't like Zeus.

But then my colleague Mark reminded me (thank God), when we were looking at the text, that glory in the gospel of John isn't quite what you might usually think glory is. In fact, it might as well be a different word, it's so different.

John says: "We have seen God's glory in the Word become flesh." Well that's kind of a crazy thing to say. It's sort of the opposite of what you'd expect anyone to say about God's glory. It goes the opposite direction. The glory isn't in the transformation of mortal flesh into divine majesty, but in the majesty becoming flesh, the big thing getting little. The big divine omniscience, omnipresence, omnipotence getting human, limited, flesh, mortal. The thing that is out there, far away, above it all, getting the same as all, close. The thing that's dry, ephemeral, clean, majestic becoming flesh. Flesh. That's blood and bones and veins and skin. That's a tongue and teeth. That's wild. That's the glory of God in the gospel of John. We have seen God's glory in the Word become flesh.

And still more different, when Jesus prays to God here to "glorify me," he means raise me up on the cross. Lift me up to be crucified. That's glory in John's gospel—the cross. That's glory? That's really freaking different. A crucifixion was a long drawn out process of public humiliation. Each step systematically deprived the one being crucified of honor and power. It was a kind of entertainment for the crowds to come and mock and ridicule the dying person.

Obviously this isn't quite the glory of the champion hockey team hero. There's something here about losing. Obviously the glory isn't the same sort of glory the queen in Snow White is after, checking the mirror, making sure she's the fairest. This is more like hurling a huge boulder at the mirror. This is not Zeus all mad because someone didn't admire his muscles sufficiently. This is God giving up all the muscle. And this is the glory of God. It doesn't exactly shine, it bleeds.

That's so insane. That's John. Glory how we usually think of it, how it's defined in the usual way (in the dictionary even), is so much about being distinct. Distinctly beautiful, or amazing, or smart. Glory is about being separated out from the ordinary herd for some outstanding quality. It's about breaking away. God's glory goes in the precise opposite direction. The glory Jesus prays for is that "they may be one as I and the Father are one." They are "in" each other, and he prays that we might be "in" him and he "in" us. It's all really very intimate sounding. It's certainly about union, not separation. The glory is in the uniting. It's not the champion winner taking his place on the highest tier. It's the father with the son. It's God with us. The glory is in the uniting, not standing apart but standing together.

We're weird beings.

I think we want glory (the our world sort of glory, the being the greatest sort of glory) because we want love. We want everyone to love us, the great big love, union. But our methods, our systems for getting glory, our whole idea of glory, sort of works in the wrong direction if what we're really aiming for, longing for, is the great big love reunion.

Our glory system works according to merit. Right? You get the glory by being smarter, or wiser, or cuter, or nicer, or having better politics or being faster, or more righteous, or a better Buddhist, or a better Christian, or stronger, or healthier, or more ethical, more environmentally aware, just more better than most people, or at least some people sometime, somehow. The glory goes to the one who has distinguished oneself, to the "winner."

So we check the queen's magic mirror to exhaustion, subtly, maybe unconsciously even. It may be in our genes. It may be survival of the fittest. But on some days, in some situations we're probably there every half hour: "Mirror mirror on the wall, how am I doing? Am I out ahead? Am I getting behind?" I don't know if we like it, but we seem to be pretty attached to, or confined by our system of glory. I don't think we believe very much really that we're saved by grace, loved, accepted into the bosom of God, made all right, completed, healed, by grace.

We act pretty much like we're pretty convinced that we're saved, loved, accepted into the bosom of God, made all right, completed, healed by the glory we merit, by our works, what we do, and not really at all by the grace of God. I think we might have a pretty big problem with grace, actually, that runs deep. We're so immersed in our glory system that grace is sort of offensive.

The Pharisees, who had quite a glory system, were so offended by the disruption that Jesus caused in their system of getting glory, felt so insulted by the suggestion that it was by grace they were saved, that they needed to kill him. And what is so offensive about grace, I wonder, the glory of God, which is so not the kind of glory we're used to. What's so offensive?

The story here, in the Bible, the story of the fall, the gospel, the whole thing, seems to say, that it's offensive because it implies we can't do it by ourselves. Because grace implies need and we don't like being needy. It's scary and we don't trust that there's really anything, anyone, anyway to provide for it, our need. It seems like *needy* to us implies inadequate, weak, bad. We want relationship. We want love so bad. But we just can't stand our own need.

We feel safer with our glory system in place. We'd rather have that (any day), than to rest, or fall, or stand in the arms of grace. We'd rather have our glory system than to be just out there *needing*. Needing God. So we make up this place to stand, this way to stand, believe we're autonomous selves moving ourselves through the world by our own devices, our own merit, our goodness or talent or power. We look at ourselves and the world as if it were made up of unrelated autonomous beings and things and events, separate, independent—not *one* at all, not in one another, not really in creation, not in God, but separate, on our own.

Of course it's a lie. Autonomy is complete fiction. At our core, we are very needy (and very related) creatures. You can't move through the world autonomously. You breathe, someone else feels the air on their cheek. You drop something, it falls on someone's head. You move, things shift, and mostly you have no idea and no control. It's not really something we have a choice about. We need all around all the time, every minute of our lives.

Without all the things outside of yourself, other than yourself, holding you up and sustaining you right now, you vaporize. You don't exist. You die. Your life is absolutely dependent on gravity and air and food and, I believe, God. But it seems like we just can't stand to live there.

In John, that made-up stance of alienated autonomy is "the world," and he has a huge polemic against it. It's not that "the world" is dirty or bad or immoral or human, it's that it makes this place to stand, this place of alienated autonomy, this false place. What was wrought in, and out of, and for relationship, attempts to live outside of it. Lives in the world of the merit system glory and not the grace of God, God's glory.

In some way, we sort of fail as lovers. We want it: communion, union, love, but somehow our way of getting glory ends up being alienating, severing, ex-communicating not-love. Having to win or be better-than gets us judging, drawing lines, not liking what's weak, what loses, what needs in humans. We believe deeply that the *needy* do not get love. You want to win love? You should probably hide the need. Really well. You should probably win at the glory game. We're actually not often fools for love. We are not going to humiliate ourselves by needing love.

God doesn't act like we do. God is so much a fool for love, so thoroughly, he chooses *need*. Chooses to need us. God's not so cool. God's the fool that goes up the tree after the cat. God chases, follows, goes to humiliating, dangerous, bloody lengths in pursuit of us, of love. Dies on the cross, loses, becomes the anti-champion for oneness, for relationship, for the sake of union, for love. God stretches out all around our game and breaks it to pieces, reduces it to ashes.

And that's the glory of God. God's glory is totally for us. God's glory undoes the alienation and separation our glory system churns out. It releases us to communion, to love for one another. May we live there.

Common Crow

April 14, 2002: Third Sunday of Easter

Now on that same day two of them were going to a village called Emmaus, about seven miles from Jerusalem, and talking with each other about all these things that had happened. While they were talking and discussing, Jesus himself came near and went with them, but their eyes were kept from recognizing him. And he said to them, "What are you discussing with each other while you walk along?" They stood still, looking sad. Then one of them, whose name was Cleopas, answered him, "Are you the only stranger in Jerusalem who does not know the things that have taken place there in these days?" He asked them, "What things?" They replied, "The things about Jesus of Nazareth, who was a prophet mighty in deed and word before God and all the people, and how our chief priests and leaders handed him over to be condemned to death and crucified him. But we had hoped that he was the one to redeem Israel. Yes, and besides all this, it is now the third day since these things took place. Moreover, some women of our group astounded us. They were at the tomb early this morning, and when they did not find his body there, they came back and told us that they had indeed seen a vision of angels who said that he was alive. Some of those who were with us went to the tomb and found it just as the women had said; but they did not see him." Then he said to them, "Oh, how foolish you are, and how slow of heart to believe all that the prophets have declared! Was it not necessary that the Messiah should suffer these things and then enter into his glory?" Then beginning with Moses and all the prophets, he interpreted to them the things about himself in all the scriptures. As they came near the village to which they were going, he walked ahead as if he were going on. But they urged him strongly, saying, "Stay with us, because it is almost evening and the day is now nearly over." So he went in to stay with them. When he was at the table with them, he took bread, blessed and broke it, and gave it to them. Then their eyes were opened, and they recognized him; and he vanished from their sight. They said to each other, "Were not our hearts burning within us while he was talking to us on the road, while he was opening the scriptures to us?" That same hour they got up and returned to Jerusalem; and they found the eleven and their companions gathered together. They were saying, "The Lord has risen indeed, and he has appeared to Simon!" Then they told what had happened on the road, and how he had been made known to them in the breaking of the bread. —Luke 24: 13-35

The Sunday Services Worship Planning Guide, Cycle A, suggests the church on the third Sunday of Easter should consider the question: "How do we perceive the continuing presence of the risen Lord in our reality today?"

I don't know why I could hardly even hear that question, when I read it in the worship-planner-thing, why it seemed so mild, and stiff and monotonous. Because once I thought about it, I realized what a very wild and dense question it really is. What an outrageous thing, actually, to suggest people come together to consider: "how we perceive the continuing presence of the risen Lord in our reality."

How do we "perceive?" That's huge. What is "presence" or "reality," if they can be said to exist at all. What's "the church" and does it even believe in the risen Lord? If you think you do perceive "the presence," is what you think it is, really it? Or are you misperceiving? Mistaking sentimental nostalgia, or self realization, or whiskey induced euphoria for God's living presence? And if you think you don't perceive the presence, are you misperceiving? And how do you ever know, who's ever going to tell you, and does it matter? Perception is such a slippery thing to consider.

But Friday morning was a beautiful morning. Saturday was too, but Friday was more so for me because the two days before were so dark and so wet. So wet that the river overflowed its banks and where there's usually a hay field now there's a little lake twenty yards from my back door. And I'm sitting out there on Friday morning and everything's all heightened because it's the first sunny day in what seems like forever (though it was maybe only three days). It's so warm and it's spring and all these birds are flying around, coming back from wherever. I'm seeing bluebirds and swans and all sorts of ducks that are usually never around but are there because of the little lake. And I see this large bird flying from the river toward me. I'm convinced it's an eagle or an osprey or some cool and rare thing. So I stand up all excited. I'm about to get the binoculars and the bird gets a little closer. It's flying fast. And I realize, oh. It's a crow. A crow. A common scavenger that hangs out in dumps and around dead animals that are smooshed on the road. It's not rare. It doesn't even sing. It croaks, like a frog.

This is no new thing flying in on this magnificent spring morning. It's been here the whole winter. It's been here all along. It's a crow. And even though there are no birders, nobody at all in my back yard, I'm embarrassed that I got so excited by a crow. How ridiculous. How could my perception be so inaccurate that I didn't recognize a crow?

Thinking about perception and seeing and recognition is fun, but it can be the kind of thing that makes you crazy. What we think are moments of clarity may really be moments of delusion. What we think is delusion may be a more accurate perception of reality (if such a thing exists). What we think is a misperceiving, may be a perceiving. We may be at our cloudiest when we're convinced about something and at our clearest when we feel cloudy.

Maybe I didn't really actually misperceive when I got excited about the crow. Maybe I was actually seeing more, not accurately, but more truthfully. Instead of the usual "it's just a crow," I saw something...stunning. The commonest, most mundane, most every day of birds, here all the time everywhere, so pervasively present that I usually don't even look at them, but I saw it. And it was, for once, for a moment...stunning. Maybe my misperception was actually a recognition of what I am, most the time, missing.

The scripture for tonight is about misperception, hiddenness, and recognition. Not seeing and seeing. The story is about the first appearance "of the risen Lord" in Luke. Some disciples are walking on a road leading out of town, maybe going home, maybe trying to leave it all behind. But they're talking about Jesus and the crucifixion, what happened, what it all means. And then, out of nowhere, the supposedly dead Jesus is present walking right on down the road beside them.

Why, I don't know, but although they are seemingly totally absorbed in his story, they don't even notice him there, present, beside them. And then even when they do look him straight in the face they don't recognize him. Maybe he's disguised or hidden. Maybe it's something totally screwed up about their vision. Maybe both, but they don't perceive the presence of the risen Lord. The text says: "Their eyes were kept from recognizing him."

Well, that seems to me about the best description I can imagine of "how we perceive the presence of the risen Lord in our lives." Not very well. Not very easily. Hardly at all. If it's there most people, most of the time, must not recognize it. The living Lord is hard to see.

Why would it ever be that God is so hidden? It's not just on the road to Emmaus. Half the Bible is about people *not seeing,* not getting it, not recognizing God. And the other half is about God hiding, in a burning bush, in clouds. God actually speaks through an ass at some point in the Old Testament. You can't see God's face and live.

Maybe people look Jesus in the face, but still nobody ever sees him clearly. None of the disciples ever do. There's always mystery, ambiguity, hiddenness. If anything's clear from the scripture, from experience, from life, from everything it's that if we do have some ongoing relationship with a living God, it's a matter of faith, not clear sight. There's always a sense that it is hidden, that our eyes are kept from any sort of constant recognition. Now you see it, now you don't.

You might think that it wouldn't be this way. If there's a God, surely that God would see to it that we recognized the living God, the risen Lord with clarity and certainty and no chance for misperception. But that's just not how it goes.

Jesus has risen from the dead in this story. God has just revealed through him that there's no obstacle to God's love, not even death, and these guys on the road don't know it, can't see it. They're all puzzled and worried and disappointed and full of despair. And they're thinking, maybe he wasn't really the messiah after all. Maybe there's no such thing as God's love.

You'd think Jesus would seize the moment to triumphantly reveal himself. Skip ahead, tear off the disguise, "Hey guys! Surprise! I'm alive. Be happy. It's me. Here I am. I'm not only the messiah, I'm God and I defeated death. Worship me. Recognize me. I'm the greatest freaking thing in the world. I have just accomplished the greatest act of love that the world will ever know. Look at me. See it." But that's just so not how Jesus operates in any of these stories.

I hate it when I go up to people that I totally assume should know me, that I've met a thousand times, and they look at me blankly, and totally do not recognize me. It's insulting to me, a little humiliating. But it doesn't seem like Jesus has such a great need to be recognized. Or there's no hurry. God seems incredibly relaxed about recognition. Incredibly patient, like there's all the time in the world and beyond the world and if not now and if not later, then, eventually.

Jesus doesn't seem worried about not being recognized in this story. He seems actually playful, the joker man, trickster. He sort of sneaks up to the disciples walking down the road, slips in beside them and plays around a little. He says, "Hey, what are you guys talking about?" They look at him and ask him, "What? Are you the only one who doesn't know about all these things?" Well, of course, he knows about all these things. He knows more than they could ever know. He knows exactly what they're talking about but he's like, "What things?"

Depending on your perspective, you could think: how sneaky, how deceptive, or you could think: how relaxed, how playful, maybe Jesus has a little sense of humor. At any rate you have to hope he does, because then these totally uncomprehending guys who don't even recognize the presence of the living Lord proceed to explain to the living Lord all about how he died and what it means and who he was. They act like know-it-alls but they know nothing, don't know him, though they're looking him in the face. But they're going to tell Jesus all about Jesus. That's probably what the church is like. It's the kind of thing that makes you want to cringe. It's embarrassing.

Jesus does call them fools, and slow to believe, but apparently that's not any sort of blanket condemnation (he's actually been a fool himself). Apparently it's not any sort of rejection because next, he goes with them, wherever it is they're going, to spend the night. When they get there they have a meal. And Jesus takes the bread. And he blesses it. And he breaks it. And he gives it to them. And they recognize him. Their eyes are opened. They finally become aware of his presence in the breaking of the bread. Jesus is finally recognized fully...in food. Weird, isn't it? It's so surprisingly physical.

Earlier, on the road, Jesus interpreted for them in the scripture all the things concerning himself. You'd think maybe when they saw that, got it intellectually, theologically, through scripture, that would have been the moment of recognition. But it's not then that they perceive his presence. Instead the recognition comes when he feeds them actual food. And not even fancy food, just bread. It seems so basic, so animal, so lowest common denominator, so everyday mundane everywhere common. Like a crow.

The words in this story—he took, blessed, broke, gave—remind us of the last supper. They are also the exact words used in an earlier story, where Jesus fed an enormous, hungry crowd. In that story there are five thousand people who can't possibly be fed with five loaves and two fish so the disciples are ready to send all the people off to find food for themselves. But quietly, without really anybody knowing the miracle of it all, Jesus breaks the bread and feeds everybody. The crowd doesn't really recognize that this was an act of the living God. They don't perceive what has happened, but they have been cared for, fed, loved by God.

Maybe that's a little like the presence of the risen Lord, the living God, in our lives. Maybe we don't see it most of the time but nevertheless God's sustaining everybody, all of creation, feeding us, loving us in some real underlying big way.

Maybe it's hidden because grace and love and mercy and hope aren't the kind of things you can perceive like you perceive other things: laws, science, math, death, words, pictures. Maybe you can't receive them like you receive moral guidance. Or accept them like you accept arguments or proof. Maybe it's "hidden" because you don't receive love and mercy and hope by being persuaded or convinced or coerced. That's not how it happens. That's not what love is like. Maybe receiving it is more like...eating bread. I'm not saying I know what that means, I'm just saying maybe it is.

What is the living God's presence in the world and how do we know it, perceive it, recognize it? I think a lot of the time we don't. It's so big, or so little, or so pervasive, or something that we can stare it in the face and not recognize it. It's hidden right before our eyes.

In the same exact second they recognize the presence of the risen Lord in this story, he vanishes from their sight. Now you see it, now you don't. You glimpse it and then it's gone. And you forget it and don't recognize it and just get all busy with paying bills and buying cars and trying to be recognized and making beds and whatever. But maybe part of the hiddenness is just that God can wait and wait and wait to be recognized, has no need to be coercive, is more concerned with getting everyone fed, sustaining love, than being recognized.

I don't know how or when or even if we perceive the presence of the risen Lord in our lives. But I believe it surrounds us, is here all the time everywhere, is pervasively present, stays the whole winter, has been here all along. May you receive it in the breaking of the bread. If not now, if not later, then, eventually. Amen.